THE WAYWARD TOURIST

THE WAYWARD TOURIST

Mark Twain's
Adventures in Australia

INTRODUCTION BY DON WATSON

MELBOURNE
UNIVERSITY
PRESS

Material in this book retains original spellings and imperial measurements
1 foot = 0.30 metres
1 mile = 1.61 kilometres
33.8 degrees Fahrenheit = 1 degree Celsius

MELBOURNE UNIVERSITY PRESS
An imprint of Melbourne University Publishing Limited
187 Grattan Street, Carlton, Victoria 3053, Australia
mup-info@unimelb.edu.au
www.mup.com.au

First published 2006
Reprinted 2006
Paperback edition published 2007
Introduction © Don Watson 2006
Illustrations by Will Goodwin
Design and typography © Melbourne University Publishing Ltd 2006

This book is copyright. Apart from any use permitted under the *Copyright Act 1968* and subsequent amendments, no part may be reproduced, stored in a retrieval system or transmitted by any means or process whatsoever without the prior written permission of the publishers.

Every attempt has been made to locate the copyright holders for material quoted in this book. Any person or organisation that may have been overlooked or misattributed should please contact the publishers.

Designed by Alice Graphics
Typeset in ITC New Baskerville by J&M Typesetting
Printed in Australia by Griffin Press

National Library of Australia Cataloguing-in-Publication entry:

Twain, Mark, 1835–1910.
The wayward tourist: Mark Twain's adventures in Australia.

Paperback ed.
ISBN 978 0 522 85431 2 (pbk.)

1. Twain, Mark, 1835–1910—Travel—Australia. 2. Authors, American—19th century—Biography. 3. Humorists, American—19th century—Biography. 4. Australia—Description and travel. I. Watson, Don. II. Title.

818.4

Contents

	Introduction	vii
1.	New, Startling Australia	1
2.	Intemperance Everywhere	13
3.	Sydney—English City with American Trimmings	19
4.	A Large Dream	26
5.	Cecil Rhodes' Shark and His First Fortune	32
6.	Bad Health—To Melbourne	45
7.	Wagga-Wagga—The Tichborne Claimant	51
8.	The Australian Larrikin—Is He Dead?	58
9.	To Adelaide	66
10.	Everything Comes to Him Who Waits	72
11.	The Laughing Jackass	82
12.	An Accurate Judgment of an Idiot	91
13.	Pudding with Arsenic Revenge	100
14.	Dodging Balls	111
15.	The Bird with a Forgettable Name	122
16.	Ballarat and the Great Nuggets	130
17.	The Mark Twain Club	139
18.	The Conciliator	151
19.	When the Moment Comes the Man Appears	164
20.	A Parrot with an Acquired Taste	175
	Afterword	183
	Notes	188

Introduction

Don Watson

In the last decade of the nineteenth century Mark Twain was the most famous man in the United States; the 'most conspicuous', to use his own words. For conspicuousness *worldwide*, he had no rival except perhaps Gladstone or Kipling, but Gladstone and Kipling could not rival his other claim to fame. For not only was Mark Twain near enough the most famous man on earth, in general he was held to be the funniest. That he was known as a funny man did not always please him, and his wife and children were adamant that 'humorist' was less exalted than their man deserved. But humour was his genius and his bread and butter and his way of coping with the gloom that dogged him. His writing amused millions and at times his public lectures generated something very like hysteria. In packed halls the slight man with the shock of hair (it was auburn in his youth) and big moustache stood quite still next to a small table on the stage and, by simply talking and looking and pausing, created unstoppable, roaring waves of laughter and groans from people with the stitch.

He could do it to roughneck audiences in California and to stuffed shirts in the east and to all the varieties of society in between. He could do it in

London and in Paris, and he could do it just as well to the common and anonymous as he could to the most revered. After sitting through one of his speeches in Chicago, the formidably unsmiling Civil War general and US President Ulysses S Grant, told Twain he had made every bone in his body ache; and observing him from a distance over a shipboard dinner Mary Mason Fairbanks wondered what gift this man possessed to make 'venerable divines and sage-looking men convulse[d] with laughter at his drolleries and quaint original manners'.

There was more behind the spell he cast than his genius with words. He was a performer, a performing artist. He refined and rehearsed his lectures until he knew each phrase and its intonation by heart and could perform them with ease in his magical—a genteel listener said 'abominable'—drawl. He claimed his sight was 'of the telescopic sort' and used it to fix on certain people in the hall—an eye Bret Harte said was 'so eagle-like a second lid would not have surprised me'. He told what he called 'humorous' stories, as distinct from the 'comic' story which was English and the 'witty' story which was French. Any fool, he said, could tell the English and French kinds because they relied only on the matter of the story, but the American form depended for its effect upon the telling, and the telling was 'a high and delicate art'. An artist knew the trick was to tell it 'gravely' and 'conceal the fact that he even dimly suspects that there is anything funny about it'. The humorous story was a rambling thing and full of incongruities of the kind made famous by Mark Twain's legendary predecessor, Artemus Ward:

'I once knew a man in New Zealand who hadn't a tooth in his head' (long reflective pause—then, dreamily) 'and yet that man could beat a drum better than any man I ever saw'. Pauses were essential, pauses of exactly the right length. Mark Twain had pauses of all lengths from short to the nearly unendurable that he would break with some drollery—his 'snapper'—that released the tension and the tide of cackles. He *worked* his audience.

Half of it was in the technique, half in the content. Knowing himself, he knew that the true humorist was a serious person if not a downright doleful one and that his stories depended for effect on the audience sensing this about him. 'The secret source of humor itself is not joy but sorrow,' he said. 'There is no humor in heaven.' His public performances were never without moments of pathos. He might, for instance, read from *Huck Finn* the scene on the river when Huck decides not to send Jim back to slavery, and lumps would form in two thousand throats—all of them to be dissolved in the next, invariably funny, story. It is possible that by these seemingly effortless combinations Mark Twain led his audience to feel that they were in the presence of not just a great artist but a great soul—and 'every bosom returned an echo', as Dr Johnson said.

Mark Twain was America's first great star, and he had a star's temperament. He threw tantrums like any other prima donna and then disliked himself for doing it. He was sensitive to criticism. Signs of disrespect, such as a patron leaving his hat on, could enrage him. But he delighted people and delighted in delighting them. One of the funniest things he ever wrote was an imaginary conversation between Elizabeth I, Walter Raleigh, Francis Bacon, Shakespeare and other Tudor luminaries. It was written in cod Elizabethan and called *1601: Conversation as It Was by the Social Fireside, in the Time of the Tudors* and among its main subjects were flatulence and sex. On their walks together Mark Twain and the Presbyterian Reverend Joe H Twichell would read it aloud to each other and end up laughing and rolling on the ground.

To please his wife or mother, or a muscular Protestant of the Joe Twichell kind, he could pretend to religious belief, but only with difficulty and it never lasted. Mark Twain was a disappointment to religion. He knew his Bible: raised a Presbyterian by his devout mother, he learned it as the Word of God, and all his life he drew on it for both material and style. He had charisma and gifts of insight, observation and persuasion for which most preachers would give their teeth. But he came to think that the Word of God was mainly claptrap and full of obscenities, unprovoked malice and irresistible inducements, he said, to juvenile masturbation. The grace his talents sometimes seemed to give him was attended always by anger and disappointment in both God and humankind.

Nothing riled him like the hypocrisy of Christians. The motto 'In God We Trust' he said, 'is simple, direct, gracefully phrased; it always sounds well ... I don't believe it would sound any better if it were true'. Though he hounded the churches he was not opposed to the *idea* of them. 'We *must* have a religion', his hero says in *A Connecticut Yankee in King Arthur's Court*, but far better to have it 'in a split up and scattered condition'. Such churches exercising an independent conscience made for a healthier republic, but churches that had become allies of worldly power and privilege were not only gross hypocrites but a threat to democratic society. As for an established church, 'any established church is an established crime', he said.

> She [the Church] invented 'the divine right of kings,' and propped it all around, brick by brick, with the Beatitudes—wrenching them from their good purpose to make them fortify an evil one; she preached (to the commoner) humility, obedience to superiors, the beauty of self sacrifice; she preached (to the commoner) meekness under insult; preached (still to the commoner, always to the commoner) patience, meanness of spirit, non-resistance under oppression; and she introduced heritable ranks and aristocracies, and taught all the Christian populations of the earth to bow down to them and worship them.

If the churches offended his moral and democratic sensibilities, as he grew older the very idea of God wounded his common sense and added insult to the injuries done to innocent people, he among them in his misery after the deaths of his wife and children. After his first and favourite daughter died he wrote: 'God gives you a wife and children whom you adore only that through the spectacle of the miseries he will inflict upon them he may tear the palpitating heart out of your breast and slap you in the face with it'. It was less that he did not believe in God's existence and more that he could not forgive Him for His crimes. Twain was halfway between a modern existentialist and the first one, Job. But in the end he was less amenable to comfort than Job. In his last work he wrote as Satan, and by then he was calling the Beatitudes 'these immense sarcasms'.

Mark Twain was born (two months prematurely) Samuel Langhorne Clemens, son of Marshall and Jane, in Florida, Missouri, on 30 November, 1835, and grew up genteel poor in Hannibal, a port on the Mississippi. Missouri was a slave state and Sam's father, a Virginian by birth and hopeless with money, owned at least two slaves and his uncle several more. The perennially cash-strapped Marshall sold the last of his, Jenni, when Sam was about seven years old. Marshall died four years later, at which point, so Sam said on his seventieth birthday in New York, his son began smoking in public (before that he had been 'discreet' about it). A feeble infant who was not expected to survive more than a few months, for the first seven years, he said, he lived 'entirely on allopathic medicine', in particular cod liver oil. The family had come into nine barrels of the stuff when his father took a drugstore for a debt and ' … it lasted me seven years. Then I was weaned'.

The place of Sam's childhood and youth lived in his mind for the rest of his life. Hannibal and the Mississippi provided the setting for *Huckleberry Finn*, and much else in all the forms and branches of his work reveals the indelible imprint it made on him. Along with his eagle eye he had a hypersensitive ear: one, he maintained, that could not stand cuckoo clocks, church bells, opera or the German language, but served him fabulously in most other things. From his memory of those river days he brought forth hosts of characters, incidents, scenes, smells, and, most tellingly perhaps, sounds—among them, voices, especially the voices of the slaves. As much as anything else it was his recreation of the American vernacular that made his writing so distinctive and influential. Through that acute ear he managed to make the world speak for itself, and do it intimately. There was the world of white Americans like Huck Finn, who begins his tale: 'You don't know about me, without you have read a book by the name of *The Adventures of Tom Sawyer*, but that ain't no matter'. There was the world of black Americans, like the teller of the ghost story he related hundreds of times, *The Golden Arm*: 'Once 'pon a time dey wuz a monsus mean man, en he live 'way out in de prairie all 'lone by hisself, 'cep'n he had a wife. En bimeby she died ... ' And there was the grand assumption behind the method: that the United States was vast and various and had to be represented in its own voice and on its own terms: 'You tell me whar a man gits his corn pone, en I'll tell you what his 'pinions is'.

And from the river came his pen name: Mark Twain means 'mark two', the 'two' meaning 'two fathoms', meaning, on a paddle steamer of the kind that for a time the young Sam Clemens piloted, 'the river is twelve feet deep, which was the safe minimum for navigation. In his first novel, *The Gilded Age,* he quotes his own conceit: one of the leadsmen on decks calls, 'By the mark twain!'

It was a commonplace among those who knew him that Mark Twain was able to say and do things that Sam Clemens was not. Later analysts argued that unintentionally or not, the name spoke for the contradictions in Sam's character, or his desire to escape from them, or from realities he feared, despised or found unbearable. All his life it was but a very short step between truth and fantasy, dream and reality. He was impressed by RL Stephenson's *Dr Jekyll and Mr Hyde* for its exploration of the dual personality of which he thought himself possessed. Reading William James on consciousness strengthened his belief in the reality of dreams, especially his own. He was 'acquainted (dimly)', he said with his 'spiritualized self', which 'can detach itself and go wandering off on its own...I know that it and I are one, because we have a common memory...' This is why it is often very hard to say which of his stories, including those he told on the stage, were drawn from his memory of real events and which from those he dreamt. He was talking about the dual personality just hours before he died. By then he had pretty well decided all Creation was a kind of dream. Maybe 'Mark Twain' spoke for that too.

Four million people in the United States, one in every eight, were slaves when the Civil War began. Strangely for a slave state, when the day came Missouri chose the Union side; stranger still in view of his later opinions, Sam joined a Confederate militia. Circumstance more than pro-slavery or secessionist conviction propelled him to the southern side; nonetheless, at twenty-five he was still as he had been raised and taught, a racist and a Southerner. His membership of the ragtag company was a bit like Coleridge enlisting in the navy, except Coleridge lasted just a night and Sam a fortnight. For the whole time they were engaged in retreating (always with wet feet and then they 'ran out of umbrellas'), until the whole company 'became so fatigued we couldn't retreat any more'.

He headed west to the goldfields of Nevada and California where he failed to find his fortune, but in the newspapers of California he did find his vocation and in the mining camps and bars another lode of writer's material. For the *Alta California* and other newspapers he wrote gems about mining life, street life, the life of crime and the lack of life in religion. He wrote about San Francisco's startlingly frequent earthquakes, and occasional brilliant hoax pieces, including one about a petrified man found in the mountains, 'pensive' in attitude and welded to the rock he sat against for centuries. A Sacramento paper sent him to the Sandwich Islands from where he dispatched a series of articles and collected the material for his first series of lectures. He went back east, a 'disreputable-looking' figure on a cholera-stricken boat in 1867. He was thirty-one and well started on the way to being the famed Mark Twain, journalist, humorist and author of a story about a frog—*The Celebrated Jumping Frog of Calaveras County.*

Some writers, his erstwhile friend and lifetime rival Bret Harte among them, get on the way to fame and stumble. Sam Clemens was never going to let that happen. He had charms to match his talents, and he soon had friends and admirers where they mattered: in New York, in the New England elites, and at the 'great barbecue of corruption' in Washington DC where he worked for a Senator and came away hating politics and convinced that the hypocrisy of the American political system rivalled that of the churches. Of these friends the most important was the editor and prolific author, William Dean Howells. Howells did more than anyone else to secure the passage of Mark Twain into the higher reaches (if not the very pinnacle) of American literature, and that of Sam Clemens into eastern society. With Howells there for the next forty years he was much less likely to fall, and it is because he didn't fall that in the last quarter of the nineteenth century American literature took on its distinctive character: 'a lean, blunt, vivid chronicle of American self-invention, from the yeasty perspective of the common man', in the words of Mark Twain's most recent biographer, Ron Powers.

The view was present in his first book, an account of a voyage he took to the Holy Land and semi-sacred sites of Italy and Greece with a shipload of mainly pious pilgrims. *The Innocents Abroad* was published in 1869, and with help from a warm Howells review in the *Atlantic Monthly*, it was an instant hit. More than that, it at once established the tenor of Mark Twain's new American voice. *Innocents Abroad* was a different kind of travel writing. There were luminous descriptions of the wonderful things they saw with none of the genre's usual mush. In places from which normally awestruck platitudes tumbled forth he came up with satires. In the Church of the Holy Sepulchre he said he wept when he came across the tomb of an ancestor, Adam. He said the copies he saw amateurs making of

The Last Supper were better than Leonardo's original. And he made the road to Damascus an excuse for flaying his companions who would not travel it on the Sabbath.

It was both the first modern travel book and a kind of boisterous scouting of territory in which Henry James would soon pitch his gorgeous tent. The habit among New World travellers had been to bow down and write about the wonders of the Old World from an Old World point of view. Mark Twain wrote from a New World point of view. Wherever he went he took the same 'yeasty perspective' that he took to California or the Mississippi. He was an American and saw no need to apologise for it. It was the Old World that had some explaining to do.

Over the next twenty years Sam Clemens carved out his place in American life. He was the pre-eminent rider on the wave of American popular culture that, driven about equally by greed, newspapers and high ideals, rolled across the country after the Civil War. He was more than a rider: he was its clear and distinctive voice. He gave shape and consciousness to the age, spoke for it and against it, was both critic and exemplar. He was on one hand Mark Twain, the conscience of America and the repository of pre–Gold Rush memory. He reckoned what had followed was 'moral rot', an age that had invented 'a thousand useless luxuries, and turned them into necessities, and satisfied none of them; it has dethroned God and set up a shekel in His place'. On the other hand, he was a practical man like Hank Morgan, his *Connecticut Yankee,* and nothing if not adaptable. If success required accommodations as well as genius he could make them.

In 1872 he published *Roughing It*, accounts of his adventures out west and in the Sandwich Islands. A year later there was *The Gilded Age*, a novel written with Charles Dudley Warner to satirise the hectic, greedy times in which he lived, and for a long while prospered. There followed in rapid succession a book of short stories, the novel *The Adventures of Tom Sawyer*, and books of reportage and memory, *Old Times on the Mississippi*, *A Tramp Abroad* and *Life on the Mississippi* which some people, including Kaiser Wilhelm of Germany, told him was his best work. And all the while he kept up a steady flow of newspaper and journal articles, many of them excoriating corruption, exploitation, imperialism and racism, and many of them merely descriptive or funny.

In the course of this great creative flow he wooed, with unremitting and ingenious intensity, and finally married the frail, demure Olivia Langdon, his *Livy*. She was the daughter of Jervis Langdon, a self-made millionaire, political progressive and passionate abolitionist who, with his wife, had been among the brave people who helped thousands of runaway slaves make their way to freedom in the north on the so-called Underground Railroad. Sam Clemens' Presbyterian Church had been for slavery and contrived to find it sanctioned in the Bible. It was in revolt against this reasoning that Livy's family had abandoned the Presbyterians and set up an abolitionist Independent Congregational Church whose principal minister was Thomas K Beecher, the brother of Harriet Beecher

Stowe. While Sam never took to the Langdons' church, he found their politics agreeable: pro-slavery and unmistakably prejudiced in his antebellum youth, as Livy's devoted husband he was an unremitting critic of Jim Crow and racism pretty well everywhere.

Livy bore Sam Clemens a son (who died as an infant) and three daughters. She also bore his long absences, his explosions of rage and the troughs of his fortune. But she would not bear less than decorous prose. She was forever knocking the rough edges off him, and her daughters, who knew nothing of Missouri, tended to support her in this project. She ran her polite eye over every word he intended for publication and amended as she went. 'I hate to have your father pictured as lashing a slave boy,' she wrote in one margin. 'It's out. And my father is whitewashed,' he wrote back. She would not stand 'He left in a sweat': he made it 'He left in a hurry'. She objected to 'stench', 'breechclout' and 'awful'. 'You are steadily weakening the English tongue, Livy,' he complained. But he changed them all. It was in part to satisfy her mannerly ambitions that he abandoned his distinctive voice in the novels, *The Prince and the Pauper* and *Personal Recollections of Joan of Arc*. His children thought they were just about the best books anyone ever wrote. His public was less enthusiastic.

For all the Clemens' collective efforts, the Brahmins never quite accepted him and the literary snobs continued to label him a 'mere humorist'. But his phenomenal book sales, astute managment of publicity, his great gift for public peformance, and his investments in the booming post-war economy combined to make him very rich. Believing his publishers had exploited him, he started his own publishing company and it got off to a stupendous start with Ulysses S Grant's *Personal Memoirs*. The great general had been at best a feckless President in a corrupt age, but Sam liked him. His terse, plain prose was much more that of the General than the President. They shared certain political views: Grant despised slavery and even more he despised the slave interests who persuaded what he called 'the poor white trash' of the South that they had common cause. He had no more time for American imperialism: the Mexican war in which he won his military stripes was, he said, 'one of the most unjust ever waged'. It was 'an instance of a republic following the bad example of European monarchies'. It might have been Mark Twain speaking. Grant's book was a triumph for both of them.

Sam Clemens poured his new riches into a magnificent house in Hartford, Connecticut, and stocked it with the finest furniture and many servants. He and Livy entertained the liberal-minded wealthy and famous in grand style. He installed a billiard table and a telephone—the first, he claimed, in New England. He preferred the table. 'The billiard table is better than the doctors,' he said. The phone was no more than a 'time-saving, profanity-breeding, useful invention' and he didn't think it would catch on sufficiently to make it worth investing in the company. But in general, he could not believe his luck.

Grant's was one of two books published by Sam Clemens in 1884–85. The other was *The Adventures of Huckleberry Finn*. What Grant had done in war,

Mark Twain did in *Huck Finn*. He took slavery head on. He put a boy on raft with a slave and let him learn the astounding truth that the slave was no less a human being than he was: that you could not lash him without his feeling pain; you could not part him from his family without his grieving; you could not take his freedom without his wanting to regain it; and that you could not give him back to slavery without forfeiting your own humanity. Like Grant in the war, in *Huckleberry Finn* Mark Twain prevailed.

Louisa May Alcott said the book was not fit for children and if Mr Mark Twain could not write something more uplifting he should not write at all. Then the newspapers joined in the chorus of polite disapproval. And then, anticipating the high-minded progressives who seventy years later proscribed *Huckleberry Finn* for calling negroes 'niggers', the high-minded traditionalists of the Public Library of Concord Massachusetts declared that the book was 'trash ... more suited to the slums than to intelligent, respectable people' and they would not have it on their shelves. They have given it 'a rattling tip-top puff', said Sam Clemens, and once he got it into the papers it would sell '25,000 copies'. Broadly speaking, he was right. He managed the press superbly, as he nearly always did, and the book was a financial success. But for libraries to ban his story while keeping unabridged Bibles available for children was an irony of a very bitter kind. It didn't help that his wife and favourite daughter were ambivalent about his masterpiece. They would have liked something a little less colloquial and a little more civilised, and in this they may as well have spoken for the mandarins who would never properly acknowledge his literary achievement.

It took a later generation to see the glories of *Huckleberry Finn* and how it transformed American literature. With few exceptions, the best American writers of the next century acknowledged its pervasive influence. The most recent is Norman Mailer, who, in a less than subtle inversion, says that to read the book now is to imagine that he has borrowed from Sinclair Lewis, John Dos Passos, Steinbeck and Faulkner: that one can see the hands of Heller and Vonnegut in the irony and Bellow in the picaresque; that it has something of *Catcher in the Rye* and traces of *Deliverance*, John Wayne, Victor McLaglen and Burt Reynolds. And much of it he surmises might well be 'lifted straight from Hemingway'. To this long list Mailer might have added *The Simpsons* and *South Park*, and the 'down-home' affectations of the current US president. In fact a United States without Mark Twain is inconceivable and probably intolerable. As for Hemingway himself, he said *Huckleberry Finn* was 'the headwater of all American fiction... There was nothing before that'.

No local panjandrum in his lifetime was as odious as the foreign one, the English one, Matthew Arnold. Arnold first offended by scoffing at Grant's grammar in a review in a British journal. Mark Twain scoffed back, bringing down the house at a New York club by reading a flatulent passage of Arnold's and declaring Grant's book a masterpiece and Grant himself an imperishable American hero. A couple of years later Arnold wrote an essay called *Civilization in the United States*. Boiled down, his thesis was that no such thing existed, and never could so long as the Americans persisted with their 'glorification of the "average man"'. He referred as well to what he called, their 'addiction to the "funny man", who is a national misfortune...' Mark Twain began but never finished a reply. But he did finish a book in which England is annihilated to the last man by modern American inventiveness and weapons of mass destruction and it is possible Arnold was on his mind when he wrote it.

The book, published in 1889, was *A Connecticut Yankee in King Arthur's Court*. Though not a great commercial success, it's hard to deny that here was another 'headwater' of an emerging American consciousness. Within a couple of decades of Mark Twain's death the *Yankee* was made into a film starring that other homespun chip off the democratic block, Will Rogers, and there have been at least half a dozen other versions, including one with Bugs Bunny as the Yankee. *A Connecticut Yankee* was satire, science fiction, burlesque, Marx Brothers farce, reminiscence—and, as always, a moral fable. It was also a statement of his bleak vision, even a prophecy of the cul de sac he imagined the United States, if not mankind, had entered.

As Sam Clemens was a man of the New World and loved America and democracy so did his character, Hank Morgan. Hank even liked the sounds Sam liked and put them to the same comforting use. Finding himself trapped in the sixth century he indulges his memories of the New Haven train: 'this k'yar don't go no furder—ahh-pls, aw-rnjz, b'nanners, s-a-n-d'ches...' Hank converts King Arthur to the cause of liberal capitalist democracy and stands like Mark Twain and

General Grant against the things that spoil or threaten its perfection: ignorance, superstition, privilege, greed, cruelty, poverty and racism. In their place he gives them science, humanism, know-how, patents, newspapers, bicycles, dynamite and marketing. He gives them irresistible progress. But just when the Stars and Stripes start billowing in every reader's heart the whole thing self-propels into the farce of Armageddon: a massacre staged by good people whose technical superiority has sapped their senses. As if mesmerised by the machinery he commands, Hank Morgan becomes a prototype of a later species of American; if not quite Dr Strangelove, then Donald Rumsfeld and other modern military spokespersons: 'Of course we could not count the dead because they did not exist as individuals, but merely as homogeneous protoplasm, with alloys of iron and buttons,' says Hank.

Clemens had a great fondness for the past but his imagination was modern. He could not resist mechanical things. He studied them, bought them and invested in them. He bought a typewriter and put two typists to work on the manuscript of *Huckleberry Finn*. He bought a bicycle. When his arm grew painful from writing he bought a phonograph and dictated directly into it before abandoning the thing because 'it hasn't any gift for elaboration'. He invested in dozens of new inventions. Not all of them were duds, but the one that really mattered was. For years he poured money into the development of a typesetting machine that the inventor had convinced him would forever change the printing business. He believed that, once perfected, every newspaper in the world must have one, and it would become for the inventor and himself a veritable money-making machine. But it sank and the Clemens fortune sank with it. The family moved to Europe and exile from the financial calamity. Then his publishing company sank as well and was declared bankrupt in April 1894. Though he was required to pay only part of the debt he told the *New York Times* he would be paying '100 cents in the dollar'.

That is how Mark Twain happened to come to Australia in 1895—to pay back his debts through a lecture tour. 'I've got to mount the platform again or starve,' he said. He signed up to tour countries on five continents and give 150 performances. He started with a couple of warm-ups in Cleveland, Ohio and travelled by train to Vancouver from where he caught the steamer *Warrimoo* for Sydney. He had companions: 'Two members of my family elected to go with me. And a carbuncle'. The family members were Livy and Clara, his second daughter. Both of them were depressed by his need to become a 'mere humorist' again.

The *Warrimoo* anchored in Watsons Bay on 15 September. Soon after that the press arrived in a launch and an interview was conducted as the writer leant over the rail. A winch was operating noisily, so much that was said by one party was not heard by the other, and vice versa, but the *Sydney Morning Herald*'s representative heard enough to report that when Twain was asked for his views on Australia, he replied, 'I don't know. I'm ready to adopt any that seem handy'. Even when they heard him clearly, it was sometimes hard to say what the great humorist had actually said and what the journalists permitted themselves to imagine Mark Twain might say.

He got off to a sticky start with the newspapers. When he said he favoured free trade they said he had insulted Sir Henry Parkes who favoured protection. If Parkes took offence he did not show it and when the two men met he pressed on him a book of his notoriously bad poems. Then Mark Twain offered his now low opinion of Bret Harte, and the Australian press said that he had insulted all the Bret Harte readers of the colonies. He offered the view that there was some merit in the theories of Henry George, but he didn't think they would come to anything practical. This was also held to be bad form. So at the end of the second day he said, 'Having thoroughly established my reputation for humor by talking of politics seriously, I shall stop'.

Instead he cast a curious and generally benign eye on wherever he was taken and whatever he was told or given to read about the country. Australian readers hoping for something equivalent to de Tocqueville's timeless observations on American democracy will be disappointed. Mark Twain did not overly extend himself or his readers when he wrote about Australia. But in the discursive, eccentric, intimate account of the journey he called *Following the Equator*, he glided around the colonies like a man on roller skates, and more than a century later his prose is still fresh enough to take his readers with him, including those in need of re-enchantment with their country's past.

Introduction

The Clemenses were greeted—almost literally—like royalty, and the lectures, called 'At Homes' were triumphs. Of the first one, at the Protestant Hall in Castlereagh Street, the S*ydney Morning Herald* reported: 'The man's work and the feeling of it was endlessly in the hearts of his audience, who not only cheered but waved hats and handkerchiefs as he stepped out from behind the Stars and Stripes'. In Melbourne an archdeacon in a box seat laughed so much he 'turned scarlet and banged his walking stick on the floor'. There was the *Jumping Frog* sketch, *The Golden Arm* and for seriousness, the moment in *Huckleberry Finn* when Huck saves Jim from slavery. The *Telegraph* said he was like 'an old friend—a personal friend' whose appearance produced 'a spontaneous expression of love and admiration'. The organ of Australian radical nationalism, the *Bulletin*, was there and their reporter said Mark Twain looked like 'an amazed gum tree'. The *Bulletin's* most talented contributor, Henry Lawson, the man who for a moment promised to be Australia's own Mark Twain, went to a performance and demanded a chair at the foot of the stage because he was deaf. It was reported that he cheered and beat his stick with enthusiasm, which only makes it seem sadder—and stranger—that there is nothing anywhere to say Lawson met him face to face. Of all the comparisons to be made between Australia and the United States at the time of Mark Twain's visit, none is more instructive or dispiriting than that between the American's passionate and supple democratic philosophy and the sentimentality and jingoism that were about to consume

Henry Lawson—a comparison of their literary production is, of course, no less depressing.

JF Archibald, the *Bulletin*'s editor, did meet Mark Twain. He took him fishing and afterwards put around the story that he had employed a boy to wait out of sight on the rocks below them and attach fish to the visitor's line. In an article in 1992 Richard Hall argued it was Archibald who gave him the impossibly tall tale about Cecil Rhodes and a shark that Twain retold in his book about the tour. Mark Twain knew that the locals took it as their stern duty to pull the legs of foreigners, and it is hard to believe he would have taken such preposterous bait. But perhaps he was tired and his resistance was low. Another joker may have fooled him with the one about a Tasmanian sheep-eating parrot. Whatever it felt like then, to have made a fool of Mark Twain does not now inspire feelings of patriotic pride. Then again, in his youth Mark Twain had been capable of his own hoaxes and professed a 'democratic' view of fact and fiction. 'I could remember everything whether it happened or not,' he once said. It is possible he might have thought that by repeating the story the joke was on them. It is even possible he dreamt it. Fascinated equally by science and spiritualism, his view of dreams and reality was also 'democratic'. Like his fictions his dreams were vivid and momentous. In Sydney he had one that he remembered for the rest of his days. In it he saw that that universe 'was the physical person of God; that the vast world that we see twinkling millions of miles apart in the fields of space are the blood corpuscles in His veins; and that we and the other creatures are the microbes that charge with multitudinous life the corpuscles'.

He was ageing, tired and in pain from the carbuncle. They still had thousands of miles to go—to New Zealand and back (all those 'junior Englands'), to Ceylon, India (for more than two months) and South Africa. Wherever he went in Australia they loved him just the same, though the reports sometimes give the impression it was only partly for what he said. It was also for his consistent graciousness, and because he was Mark Twain. While he did not exactly 'give them muck' as Nellie Melba once recommended to a fellow performer, he knew the proprieties and did not trouble his Australian audiences with social criticism or question with any vigour the direction the Australian colonies were taking. He arrived at the tail end of an economic depression, a drought, rabbit plagues and the great effort for Federation, and chose the rabbits for the immortal paragraph. He had missed the very worst of the worst economic depression in Australian history by only a couple of years, but it was the prosperity and success of the place he noted, and he warmed to the egalitarian spirit. Not that he was wrong to admire the public investment in civic buildings and services; the way a town of just 40 000 people such as Ballarat 'has every essential of an advanced and enlightened big city'. As for the labouring classes, it was as if the trade unions, which were at that moment recovering from withering defeats two years earlier, had misread their situation. 'The workingman was a great power everywhere in Australia,' Mark Twain wrote. He was right in this as well, though to say that in

South Australia the worker was 'sovereign' and that South Australia was his 'paradise' was taking it a little too far. In his notebook he went even further: 'Australia is the modern heaven—it is bossed absolutely by the workingman'.

He did notice the effort for Australasian Federation and met some of the main players, among them Sir Henry Parkes. Federation had Mark Twain's blessing, but the man who so loved the American republic and loathed hereditary privilege, the established church and imperialism thought it would be 'unwise' and unnecessary for the colonies to 'cut loose from the British Empire'. He had read the mood well. The Australian colonists were in general both pragmatic and loyal, and to the extent that they supported federation they preferred it 'under the Crown'. The American colonists would have taken the same course if they had not been commercially oppressed, Mark Twain wrote. The truth is he loved England almost as much as he loved the English language. And Matthew Arnold notwithstanding, the English loved him, and he delighted in their approval. Rudyard Kipling got the Nobel Prize in 1905 but two years later Oxford gave Mark Twain a doctorate and chances are it meant as much to him.

It has always been the way and a great sadness to Australians of several generations: whenever celebrated writers, or celebrated anything, come to Australia they seem to be less interested in the people and their achievements than they are in the animals. It is surprising that Mark Twain was not photographed holding a koala. We crave his estimate of Alfred Deakin and instead find kookaburras, magpies, platypuses, boomerangs and the Melbourne Cup. Why Tasmania always gets the writers gushing forth, who can say? He spent no more than a few hours in Hobart, but this was enough for two chapters about the convict settlers and the cruelty of the system that sent them to the colonies for the pettiest misdemeanours. In Hobart he visited a home for the indigent and saw ex-convicts there: 'a crowd ... of the oldest people I have ever seen'. There are photographs of these survivors of the convict days. Not only do they look old, they look dead. They might as well be made of wax. It is not surprising that the visit seemed to leave a mark and made him think of 'life in death'. He saw no Aborigines, but he wrote more about them than everything else put together. By contemporary standards his tone was grossly patronising and as often as not he had the facts wrong. But what he said about the 'savages' was unfailingly sympathetic, curious and admiring and in this he ran hard against the local prejudice.

Perhaps inspired by Sir Henry's poems, at his third performance in Sydney Mark Twain came up with some verse. He said it was an example of how hard it is to write poetry when one knows nothing about it. It went:

> Land of the ornithorhyncus
> Land of the kangaroo
> Old ties of heredity link us

Then he stopped. This was as much as he had with him, he said. He had composed three more stanzas but had given them to a man he met on the way to the hall who said he'd had nothing to eat for two weeks. The routine created one of those roaring waves of laughter, so he repeated it in several other places. It spoke sublimely for the traveller's dilemma and somehow captured the unequal and unresolved nature of the relationship between the two countries—and it was possibly the most brilliant thing he did in Australia.

Soon after they reached London the Clemenses learned that Susy, the eldest daughter and Sam's favourite, had died of spinal meningitis. 'It is one of the mysteries of our nature that a man, all unprepared, can receive a thunderstroke like that and live,' he wrote. Livy died a few years later after long debilitating illness. Their second daughter, Jean, developed violent epilepsy and had to be placed in an institution. She died in her father's New York home a few months before he did. Sam thus outlived his wife and three of his four children. If he was America's 'greatest and most embittered humorist' as William Safire chooses to describe him, there were these good reasons. There was as well what he saw as shameful American military imperialism and the complicity of Christians—and the Christian God—in the crime. In 1906 he wrote a Swiftian denunciation called 'The War Prayer' but it was not published in his lifetime. He died in New York in 1910, the same year as Tolstoy, who might as well be called 'Russia's greatest and most embittered novelist'.

As a novelist perhaps Mark Twain does not measure up to Tolstoy, or to his countryman Henry James, or to the requirements of Matthew Arnold. Yet from the novels, stories and journalism of this 'mere humorist' flowed all of American twentieth-century realism, and that influence of course went further still. Had he replied to Arnold's jibe at any time in the last thirty years of his life he could have said that the 'funny man' was the clearest and most recognisable voice of his country, and more than those of any other writer his words and his imagination tell us what that country was like. Funniest or most embittered, he was also surely among the sanest Americans—and if he were alive now he would seem even saner. He was at once a critic of his country and its most loved citizen. That he had run away from the war that became the *sine qua non* of manly patriotism did not matter. That he lived for long periods in Britain and Europe did not reduce him in his compatriots' famously provincial eyes or dim his understanding of them. That he was a Southerner, a secularist, an anti-imperialist, an anti-racist and an ironist in an age when evangelical religion, the Monroe Doctrine, Jim Crow and undiluted patriotism were ascendant creeds did not matter. He remained the essential American and the still small voice of the flimsy, paradoxical, eternal good in the democracy. For most of those who have read him he still is. The trick, as he said, was all in the telling.

The Wayward Tourist publishes edited extracts from Mark Twain's *Following the Equator* (1897).

1

New, Startling Australia

*It is your human environment that
makes climate.*

—*Pudd'nhead Wilson's New Calendar*

Sept. 15—*Night.* Close to Australia now. Sydney 50 miles distant.

That note recalls an experience. The passengers were sent for, to come up in the bow and see a fine sight. It was very dark. One could not follow with the eye the surface of the sea more than fifty yards in any direction—it dimmed away and became lost to sight at about that distance from us. But if you patiently gazed into the darkness a little while, there was a sure reward for you. Presently, a quarter of a mile away you would see a blinding splash or explosion of light on the water—a flash so sudden and so astonishingly brilliant that it would make you catch your breath; then that blotch of light would instantly extend itself and take the corkscrew shape and imposing length of the fabled sea-serpent, with every curve of its body and the 'break' spreading away from its head, and the wake following behind its tail clothed in a fierce splendor of living fire. And my, but it was coming at a lightning gait! Almost before you could think, this monster of light, fifty feet long, would go flaming and storming by, and suddenly disappear. And out in the distance whence he came you would see another flash; and another and another and another, and see them turn into sea-serpents on the instant; and once sixteen flashed up at the same time and came tearing towards us, a swarm of wiggling curves, a moving conflagration, a vision of bewildering beauty, a spectacle of fire and energy whose equal the most of those people will not see again until after they are dead.

It was porpoises—porpoises aglow with phosphorescent light. They presently collected in a wild and magnificent jumble under the bows, and there they played for an hour, leaping and frollicking and carrying on, turning summersaults in front of the stem or across it and never getting hit, never making a miscalculation, though the stem missed them only about an inch, as a rule. They were porpoises of the ordinary length—eight or ten feet—but every twist of their bodies sent a long procession of united and glowing curves astern. That fiery jumble was an enchanting thing to look at, and we stayed out the performance; one cannot have such a show as that twice in a lifetime. The porpoise is the kitten of the sea; he never has a serious thought, he cares for nothing but fun and play.

But I think I never saw him at his winsomest until that night. It was near a center of civilization, and he could have been drinking.

By and by, when we had approached to somewhere within thirty miles of Sydney Heads the great electric light that is posted on one of those lofty ramparts began to show, and in time the little spark grew to a great sun and pierced the firmament of darkness with a far-reaching sword of light.

Sydney Harbor is shut in behind a precipice that extends some miles like a wall, and exhibits no break to the ignorant stranger. It has a break in the middle, but it makes so little show that even Captain Cook sailed by it without seeing it. Near by that break is a false break which resembles it, and which used to make trouble for the mariner at night, in the early days before the place was lighted. It caused the memorable disaster to the *Duncan Dunbar*, one of the most pathetic tragedies in the history of that pitiless ruffian, the sea. The ship was a sailing vessel; a fine and favorite passenger packet, commanded by a popular captain of high reputation. She was due from England, and Sydney was waiting, and counting the hours; counting the hours, and making ready to give her a heart-stirring welcome; for she was bringing back a great company of mothers and daughters, the long-missed light and bloom of life of Sydney homes; daughters that had been years absent at school, and mothers that had been with them all that time watching over them. Of all the world only India and Australasia have by custom freighted ships and fleets with their hearts, and know the tremendous meaning of that phrase; only they know what the waiting is like when this freightage is entrusted to the fickle winds, not steam, and what the joy is like when the ship that is returning this treasure comes safe to port and the long dread is over.

On board the *Duncan Dunbar*, flying toward Sydney Heads in the waning afternoon, the happy homecomers made busy preparation, for it was not doubted that they would be in the arms of their friends before the day was done; they put away their sea-going clothes and put on clothes meeter for the meeting, their richest and their loveliest, these poor brides of the grave. But the wind lost force, or there was a miscalculation, and before the Heads were sighted the darkness came on. It was said that ordinarily the captain would have made a safe offing and waited for the morning; but this was no ordinary occasion; all about him were appealing faces, faces pathetic with disappointment. So his sympathy moved him to try the dangerous passage in the dark. He had entered the Heads seventeen times, and believed he knew the ground. So he steered straight for the false opening, mistaking it for the true one. He did not find out that he was wrong until it was too late. There was no saving the ship. The great seas swept her in and crushed her to splinters and rubbish upon the rock tushes at the base of the precipice. Not one of all that fair and gracious company was ever seen again alive. The tale is told to every stranger that passes the spot, and it will continue to be told to all that come, for generations; but it will never grow old, custom cannot stale it, the heartbreak that is in it can never perish out of it.

There were two hundred persons in the ship, and but one survived the disaster. He was a sailor. A huge sea flung him up the face of the precipice and stretched him on a narrow shelf of rock midway between the top and the bottom, and there he lay all night. At any other time he would have lain there for the rest of his life, without chance of discovery; but the next morning the ghastly news swept through Sydney that the *Duncan Dunbar* had gone down in sight of home, and straightway the walls of the Heads were black with mourners; and one of these, stretching himself out over the precipice to spy out what might be seen below, discovered this miraculously preserved relic of the wreck. Ropes were brought and the nearly impossible feat of rescuing the man was accomplished. He was a person with a practical turn of mind, and he hired a hall in Sydney and exhibited himself at sixpence a head till he exhausted the output of the gold fields for that year.

We entered and cast anchor, and in the morning went oh-ing and ah-ing in admiration up through the crooks and turns of the spacious and beautiful harbor—a harbor which is the darling of Sydney and the wonder of the world. It is not surprising that the people are proud of it, nor that they put their enthusiasm into eloquent words. A returning citizen asked me what I thought of it, and I testified with a cordiality which I judged would be up to the market rate. I said it was beautiful—superbly beautiful. Then by a natural impulse I gave God the praise. The citizen did not seem altogether satisfied. He said:

'It *is* beautiful, of course it's beautiful—the Harbor; but that isn't all of it, it's only half of it; Sydney's the other half, and it takes both of them together to ring the supremacy-bell. God made the Harbor, and that's all right; but Satan made Sydney.'

Of course I made an apology; and asked him to convey it to his friend. He was right about Sydney being half of it. It would be beautiful without Sydney, but not above half as beautiful as it is now, with Sydney added. It is shaped somewhat like an oak-leaf—a roomy sheet of lovely blue water, with narrow off-shoots of water running up into the country on both sides between long fingers of land, high wooden ridges with sides sloped like graves. Handsome villas are perched here and there on these ridges, snuggling amongst the foliage, and one catches alluring glimpses of them as the ship swims by toward the city. The city clothes a cluster of hills and a ruffle of neighboring ridges with its undulating masses of masonry, and out of these masses spring towers and spires and other architectural dignities and grandeurs that break the flowing lines and give picturesqueness to the general effect.

The narrow inlets which I have mentioned go wandering out into the land everywhere and hiding themselves in it, and pleasure-launches are always exploring them with picnic parties on board. It is said by trustworthy people that if you explore them all you will find that you have covered 700 miles of water passage. But there are liars everywhere this year, and they will double that when their works are in good going order.

October was close at hand, spring was come. It was really spring—everybody said so; but you could have sold it for summer in Canada, and nobody would have suspected. It was the very weather that makes our home summers the perfection of climatic luxury; I mean, when you are out in the wood or by the sea. But these people said it was cool, now—a person ought to see Sydney in the summer time if he wanted to know what warm weather is; and he ought to go north ten or fifteen hundred miles if he wanted to know what hot weather is. They said that away up there toward the equator the hens laid fried eggs. Sydney is the place to go to get information about other people's climates. It seems to me that the occupation of Unbiased Traveler Seeking Information is the pleasantest and most irresponsible trade there is. The traveler can always find out anything he wants to, merely by asking. He can get at all the facts, and more. Everybody helps him, nobody hinders him. Anybody who has an old fact in stock that is no longer negotiable in the domestic market will let him have it at his own price. An accumulation of such goods is easily and quickly made. They cost almost nothing and they bring par in the foreign market. Travelers who come to America always freight up with the same old nursery tales that their predecessors selected, and they carry them back and always work them off without any trouble in the home market.

If the climates of the world were determined by parallels of latitude, then we could know a place's climate by its position on the map; and so we should know that the climate of Sydney was the counterpart of the climate of Columbia, S. C. and of Little Rock, Arkansas, since Sydney is about the same distance south of the equator that those other towns are north of it—thirty-four degrees. But no, climate disregards the parallels of latitude. In Arkansas they have a winter; in Sydney they have the name of it, but not the thing itself. I have seen the ice in the Mississippi floating past the mouth of the Arkansas river; and at Memphis, but a little way above, the Mississippi has been frozen over, from bank to bank. But they have never had a cold spell in Sydney which brought the mercury down to freezing point. Once in a mid-winter day there, in the month of July, the mercury went down to 36°, and that remains the memorable 'cold day' in the history of the town. No doubt Little Rock has seen it below zero. Once, in Sydney, in mid-summer, about New Year's Day, the mercury went up to 106° in the shade, and that is Sydney's memorable hot day. That would about tally with Little Rock's hottest day also, I imagine. My Sydney figures are taken from a government report, and are trustworthy. In the matter of summer weather Arkansas has no advantage over Sydney, perhaps, but when it comes to winter weather, that is another affair. You could cut up an Arkansas winter into a hundred Sydney winters and have enough left for Arkansas and the poor ...

But Nature is always stingy of perfect climates; stingier in the case of Australia than usual. Apparently this vast continent has a really good climate nowhere but around the edges.

If we look at a map of the world we are surprised to see how big Australia is. It is about two-thirds as large as the United States was before we added Alaska.

But where as one finds a sufficiently good climate and fertile land almost everywhere in the United States, it seems settled that inside of the Australian border-belt one finds many deserts and in spots a climate which nothing can stand except a few of the hardier kinds of rocks. In effect, Australia is as yet unoccupied. If you take a map of the United States and leave the Atlantic seaboard States in their places; also the fringe of Southern States from Florida west to the Mouth of the Mississippi; also a narrow, inhabited streak up the Mississippi half-way to its head waters; also a narrow, inhabited border along the Pacific coast: then take a brushful of paint and obliterate the whole remaining mighty stretch of country that lies between the Atlantic States and the Pacific-coast strip, your map will look like the latest map of Australia.

This stupendous blank is hot, not to say torrid; a part of it is fertile, the rest is desert; it is not liberally watered; it has no towns. One has only to cross the mountains of New South Wales and descend into the westward-lying regions to find that he has left the choice climate behind him, and found a new one of a quite different character. In fact, he would not know by the thermometer that he was not in the blistering Plains of India. Captain Sturt, the great explorer, gives us a sample of the heat.

> The wind, which had been blowing all the morning from the N.E., increased to a heavy gale, and I shall never forget its withering effect. I sought shelter behind a large gum-tree, but the blasts of heat

were so terrific that I wondered *the very grass did not take fire.* This really was nothing ideal: everything both animate and inanimate gave way before it; the horses stood with their backs to the wind and their noses to the ground, without the muscular strength to raise their heads; the birds were mute, and the leaves of the trees under which we were sitting *fell like a snow shower around us.* At noon I took a thermometer graded to 127°, out of my box, and observed that the mercury was up to 125°. Thinking that it had been unduly influenced, I put it in the fork of a tree close to me, sheltered alike from the wind and the sun. I went to examine it about an hour afterwards, when I found the mercury had risen to the top of the instrument and had *burst the bulb,* a circumstance that I believe no traveler has ever before had to record. I cannot find language to convey to the reader's mind an idea of the intense and oppressive nature of the heat that prevailed.

That hot wind sweeps over Sydney sometimes, and brings with it what is called a 'dust-storm.' It is said that most Australian towns are acquainted with the dust-storm. I think I know what it is like, for the following description by Mr. Gane tallies very well with the alkali dust-storm of Nevada, if you leave out the 'shovel' part. Still the shovel part is a pretty important part, and seems to indicate that my Nevada storm is but a poor thing, after all.

As we proceeded the altitude became less, and the heat proportionately greater until we reached

Dubbo, which is only 600 feet above sea-level. It is a pretty town, built on an extensive plain . . . After the effects of a shower of rain have passed away the surface of the ground crumbles into a thick layer of dust, and occasionally, when the wind is in a particular quarter, *it is lifted bodily from the ground in one long opaque cloud.* In the midst of such a storm nothing can be seen a few yards ahead, and the unlucky person who happens to be out at the time is compelled to seek the nearest retreat at hand. When the thrifty housewife sees in the distance the dark column advancing in a steady whirl towards her house, she closes the doors and windows with all expedition. A drawing-room, the window of which has been carelessly left open during a dust-storm, is indeed an extraordinary sight. A lady who has resided in Dubbo for some years says that the dust lies so thick on the carpet that it is necessary to use a shovel to remove it.

And probably a wagon. I was mistaken; I have not seen a proper dust-storm. To my mind the exterior aspects and character of Australia are fascinating things to look at and think about, they are so strange, so weird, so new, so uncommonplace, such a startling and interesting contrast to the other sections of the planet, the sections that are known to us all, familiar to us all. In the matter of particulars—a detail here, a detail there—we have had the choice climate of New South Wales' sea-coast; we have had the Australian heat as furnished by Captain Sturt; we have had the wonderful dust-storm; and we have considered the phenomenon of an almost empty hot wilderness half as big as the United States, with a narrow belt of civilization, population, and good climate around it.

2

Intemperance Everywhere

> Everything human is pathetic. The secret
> source of Humor itself is not joy but
> sorrow. There is no humor in heaven.
>
> —*Pudd'nhead Wilson's New Calendar*

Captain Cook found Australia in 1770, and eighteen years later the British Government began to transport convicts to it. Altogether, New South Wales received 83,000 in 53 years. The convicts wore heavy chains; they were ill-fed and badly treated by the officers set over them; they were heavily punished for even slight infractions of the rules; 'the cruelest discipline ever known' is one historian's description of their life.[1]

English law was hard-hearted in those days. For trifling offenses which in our day would be punished by a small fine or a few days' confinement, men, women, and boys were sent to this other end of the earth to serve terms of seven and fourteen years; and for serious crimes they were transported for life. Children were sent to the penal colonies for seven years for stealing a rabbit!

When I was in London twenty-three years ago there was a new penalty in force for diminishing garroting and wife-beating—25 lashes on the bare back with the cat-o'-nine-tails. It was said that this terrible punishment was able to bring the stubbornest ruffians to terms; and that no man had been found with grit enough to keep his emotions to himself beyond the ninth blow; as a rule the man shrieked earlier. That penalty had a great and wholesome effect upon the garroters and wife-beaters; but humane modern London could not endure it; it got its law rescinded. Many a bruised and battered English wife has since had occasion to deplore that cruel achievement of sentimental 'humanity.'

Twenty-five lashes! In Australia and Tasmania they gave a convict fifty for almost any little offense; and sometimes a brutal officer would add fifty, and then another fifty, and so on, as long as the sufferer could endure the torture and live. In Tasmania I read the entry, in an old manuscript official record, of a case where a convict was given *three hundred* lashes—for stealing some silver spoons. And men got more than that, sometimes. Who handled the cat? Often it was another convict; sometimes it was the culprit's dearest comrade; and he had to lay on with all his might; otherwise he would get a flogging himself for his mercy—for he was under watch—and yet not do his friend any good: the friend would be attended to by another hand and suffer no lack in the matter of full punishment.

The convict life in Tasmania was so unendurable, and suicide so difficult to accomplish that once or twice despairing men got together and drew straws to determine which of them should kill another of the group—this murder to secure death to the perpetrator and to the witnesses of it by the hand of the hangman!

The incidents quoted above are mere hints, mere suggestions of what convict life was like—they are but a couple of details tossed into view out of a shoreless sea of such; or, to change the figure, they are but a pair of flaming steeples photographed from a point which hides from sight the burning city which stretches away from their bases on every hand.

Some of the convicts—indeed, a good many of them—were very bad people, even for that day; but the most of them were probably not noticeably worse than the average of the people they left behind them at home. We must believe this; we cannot avoid it. We are obliged to believe that a nation that could look on, unmoved, and see starving or freezing women hanged for stealing twenty-six cents' worth of bacon or rags, and boys snatched from their mothers, and men from their families, and sent to the other side of the world for long terms of years for similar trifling offenses, was a nation to whom the term 'civilized' could not in any large way be applied. And we must also believe that a nation that knew, during more than forty years, what was happening to those exiles and was still content with it, was not advancing in any showy way toward a higher grade of civilization.

If we look into the characters and conduct of the officers and gentlemen who had charge of the convicts and attended to their backs and stomachs, we must grant again that as between the convict and his masters, and between both and the nation at home, there was a quite noticeable monotony of sameness.

Four years had gone by, and many convicts had come. Respectable settlers were beginning to arrive. These two classes of colonists had to be protected, in case of trouble among themselves or with the natives. It is proper to mention the natives, though they could hardly count they were so scarce. At a time when they had not as yet begun to be much disturbed—not as yet being in the way—it was estimated that in New South Wales there was but one native to 45,000 acres of territory.

People had to be protected. Officers of the regular army did not want this service—away off there where neither honor nor distinction was to be gained. So England recruited and officered a kind of militia force of 1,000 uniformed civilians called the 'New South Wales Corps' and shipped it.

This was the worst blow of all. The colony fairly staggered under it. The Corps was an object-lesson of the moral condition of England outside of the jails. The colonists trembled. It was feared that next there would be an importation of the nobility.

In those early days the colony was non-supporting. All the necessaries of life—food, clothing, and all—were sent out from England, and kept in great government store-houses, and given to the convicts and sold to the settlers—sold at a trifling advance upon cost. The Corps saw its opportunity. Its officers went into commerce, and in a most lawless way. They went to importing rum, and also to manufacturing it in private stills, in defiance of the government's commands and protests. They leagued themselves together and ruled the market; they boycotted the government and the other dealers; they established a close monopoly and kept it strictly in their own hands. When a vessel arrived with spirits, they allowed nobody to buy but themselves, and they forced the owner to sell to them at a price named by themselves—and it was always low enough. They bought rum at an average of two dollars a gallon and sold it at an average of ten. They *made rum the currency of the country*—for there was little or no money—and they maintained their devastating hold and kept the colony under their heel for eighteen or twenty years before they were finally conquered and routed by the government.

Meantime, they had spread intemperance everywhere. And they had squeezed farm after farm out of the settlers' hands for rum, and thus had bountifully enriched themselves. When a farmer was caught in the last agonies of thirst they took advantage of him and sweated him for a drink.

In one instance they sold a man a gallon of rum worth two dollars for a piece of property which was sold some years later for $100,000.

When the colony was about eighteen or twenty years old it was discovered that the land was specially fitted for the wool culture. Prosperity followed, commerce with the world began, by and by rich mines of the noble metals were opened, immigrants flowed in, capital likewise. The result is the great and wealthy and enlightened commonwealth of New South Wales.

It is a country that is rich in mines, wool ranches, trams, railways, steamship lines, schools, newspapers, botanical gardens, art galleries, libraries, museums, hospitals, learned societies; it is the hospitable home of every species of culture and of every species of material enterprise, and there is a church at every man's door, and a race-track over the way.

3

Sydney—English City with American Trimmings

> We should be careful to get out of an experience only the wisdom that is in it —and stop there; lest we be like the cat that sits down on a hot stove-lid. She will never sit down on a hot stove-lid again —and that is well; but also she will never sit down on a cold one any more.
>
> —*Pudd'nhead Wilson's New Calendar*

All English-speaking colonies are made up of lavishly hospitable people, and New South Wales and its capital are like the rest in this. The English-speaking colony of the United States of America is always called lavishly hospitable by the English traveler. As to the other English-speaking colonies throughout the world from Canada all around, I know by experience that the description fits them. I will not go more particularly into this matter, for I find that when writers try to distribute their gratitude here and there and yonder by detail they run across difficulties and do some ungraceful stumbling.

Mr. Gane (*New South Wales and Victoria in 1885*), tried to distribute his gratitude, and was not lucky:[1]

> The inhabitants of Sydney are renowned for their hospitality. The treatment which we experienced at the hands of this generous-hearted people will help more than anything else to make us recollect with pleasure our stay amongst them. In the character of hosts and hostesses they excel. The 'new chum' needs only the acquaintanceship of one of their number, and he becomes at once the happy recipient of numerous complimentary invitations and thoughtful kindnesses. Of the towns it has been our good fortune to visit, none have portrayed home so faithfully as Sydney.

Nobody could say it finer than that. If he had put in his cork then, and stayed away from Dubbo—but no; heedless man, he pulled it again. Pulled it when he was away along in his book, and his memory of what he had said about Sydney had grown dim:

> We cannot quit the promising town of Dubbo without testifying, in warm praise, to the kind-hearted and hospitable usages of its inhabitants. Sydney, though well deserving the character it bears of its kindly treatment of strangers, possesses a little formality and reserve. In Dubbo, on the contrary,

though the same congenial manners prevail, there is a pleasing degree of respectful familiarity which gives the town a homely comfort not often met with elsewhere. In laying on one side our pen we feel contented in having been able, though so late in this work, to bestow a panegyric, however unpretentious, on a town which, though possessing no picturesque natural surroundings, nor interesting architectural productions, has yet a body of citizens whose hearts cannot but obtain for their town a reputation for benevolence and kind-heartedness.

I wonder what soured him on Sydney. It seems strange that a pleasing degree of three or four fingers of respectful familiarity should fill a man up and give him the panegyrics so bad. For he *has* them, the worst way—any one can see that. A man who is perfectly at himself does not throw cold detraction at people's architectural productions and picturesque surroundings, and let on that what he prefers is a Dubbonese dust-storm and a pleasing degree of respectful familiarity. No, these are old, old symptoms; and when they appear we know that the man has got the panegyrics.

Sydney has a population of 400,000. When a stranger from America steps ashore there, the first thing that strikes him is that the place is eight or nine times as large as he was expecting it to be; and the next thing that strikes him is that it is an English city with American trimmings. Later on, in Melbourne, he will find the American trimmings still more in evidence; there, even the architecture will often suggest America; a photograph of its stateliest business street might be passed upon him for a picture of the finest street in a large American city. I was told that the most of the fine residences were the city residences of squatters. The name seemed out of focus somehow. When the explanation came, it offered a new instance of the curious changes which words, as well as animals, undergo through change of habitat and climate. With us, when you speak of a squatter you are always supposed to be speaking of a poor man, but in Australia when you speak of a squatter you are supposed to be speaking of a millionaire; in America the word indicates the possessor of a few acres and a doubtful title, in Australia it indicates a man whose landfront is as long as a railroad, and whose title has been perfected in one way or another; in America the word indicates a man who owns a dozen head of live stock, in Australia a man who owns anywhere from fifty thousand up to half a million head; in America the word indicates a man who is obscure and not important, in Australia a man who is prominent and of the first importance; in America you take off your hat to no squatter, in Australia you do; in America if your uncle is a squatter you keep it dark, in Australia you advertise it; in America if your friend is a squatter nothing comes of it, but with a squatter for your friend in Australia you may sup with kings if there are any around.

In Australia it takes about two acres and a half of pastureland (some people say twice as many), to support a sheep; and when the squatter has half a million sheep his private domain is about as large as Rhode Island, to speak in general terms. His annual wool crop may be worth a quarter or a half million dollars.

He will live in a palace in Melbourne or Sydney or some other of the large cities, and make occasional trips to his sheep-kingdom several hundred miles away in the great plains to look after his battalions of riders and shepherds and other hands. He has a commodious dwelling out there, and if he approve of you he will invite you to spend a week in it, and will make you at home and comfortable, and let you see the great industry in all its details, and feed you and slake you and smoke you with the best that money can buy.

On at least one of these vast estates there is a considerable town, with all the various businesses and occupations that go to make an important town; and the town and the land it stands upon are the property of the squatters. I have seen that town, and it is not unlikely that there are other squatter-owned towns in Australia.

Australia supplies the world not only with fine wool, but with mutton also. The modern invention of cold storage and its application in ships has created this great trade. In Sydney I visited a huge establishment where they kill and clean and solidly freeze a thousand sheep a day, for shipment to England.

The Australians did not seem to me to differ noticeably from Americans, either in dress, carriage, ways, pronunciation, inflections, or general appearance. There were fleeting and subtle suggestions of their English origin, but these were not pronounced enough, as a rule, to catch one's attention. The people have easy and cordial manners from the beginning—from the moment that the introduction is completed. This is American. To put it in another way, it is

English friendliness with the English shyness and self-consciousness left out.

Now and then—but this is rare—one hears such words as *piper* for paper, *lydy* for lady, and *tyble* for table fall from lips whence one would not expect such pronunciations to come. There is a superstition prevalent in Sydney that this pronunciation is an Australianism, but people who have been 'home'—as the native reverently and lovingly calls England—know better. It is 'costermonger'. All over Australasia this pronunciation is nearly as common among servants as it is in London among the uneducated and the partially educated of all sorts and conditions of people. That mislaid y is rather striking when a person gets enough of it into a short sentence to enable it to show up. In the hotel in Sydney the chambermaid said, one morning—

> The tyble is set, and here is the piper; and if the lydy
> is ready I'll tell the wyter to bring up the breakfast.

I have made passing mention, a moment ago, of the native Australasian's custom of speaking of England as 'home.' It was always pretty to hear it, and often it was said in an unconsciously caressing way that made it touching; in a way which transmuted a sentiment into an embodiment, and made one seem to see Australasia as a young girl stroking mother England's old gray head.

In the Australasian home the table-talk is vivacious and unembarrassed; it is without stiffness or restraint. This does not remind one of England so much as it does of America. But Australasia is strictly democratic, and reserves and restraints are things that are bred by differences of rank.

English and colonial audiences are phenomenally alert and responsive. Where masses of people are gathered together in England, caste is submerged, and with it the English reserve; equality exists for the moment, and every individual is free; so free from any consciousness of fetters, indeed, that the Englishman's habit of watching himself and guarding himself against any injudicious exposure of his feelings is forgotten, and falls into abeyance—and to such a degree indeed, that he will bravely applaud all by himself if he wants to—an exhibition of daring which is unusual elsewhere in the world.

But it is hard to move a new English acquaintance when he is by himself, or when the company present is small, and new to him. He is on his guard then, and his natural reserve is to the fore. This has given him the false reputation of being without humor and without the appreciation of humor.

Americans are not Englishmen, and American humor is not English humor; but both the American and his humor had their origin in England, and have merely undergone changes brought about by changed conditions and a new environment. About the best humorous speeches I have yet heard were a couple that were made in Australia at club suppers—one of them by an Englishman, the other by an Australian.

4

A Large Dream

> There are those who scoff at the schoolboy, calling him frivolous and shallow. Yet it was the schoolboy who said 'Faith is believing what you know ain't so.'
>
> —*Pudd'nhead Wilson's New Calendar*

In Sydney I had a large dream, and in the course of talk I told it to a missionary from India who was on his way to visit some relatives in New Zealand. I dreamed that the visible universe is the physical person of God; that the vast worlds that we see twinkling millions of miles apart in the fields of space are the blood corpuscles in His veins; and that we and the other creatures are the microbes that charge with multitudinous life the corpuscles.

Mr. X., the missionary, considered the dream awhile, then said:

It is not surpassable for magnitude, since its metes and bounds are the metes and bounds of the universe itself; and it seems to me that it almost accounts for a thing which is otherwise nearly unaccountable—the origin of the sacred legends of the Hindoos. Perhaps they dream them, and then honestly believe them to be divine revelations of fact. It looks like that, for the legends are built on so vast a scale that it does not seem reasonable that plodding priests would happen upon such colossal fancies when awake.

He told some of the legends, and said that they were implicitly believed by all classes of Hindoos, including those of high social position and intelligence; and he said that this universal credulity was a great hindrance to the missionary in his work. Then he said something like this:

At home, people wonder why Christianity does not make faster progress in India. They hear that the Indians believe easily, and that they have a natural trust in miracles and give them a hospitable reception. Then they argue like this: since the Indian believes easily, place Christianity before them and they must believe; confirm its truths by the biblical miracles, and they will no longer doubt. The natural deduction is, that as Christianity makes but indifferent progress in India, the fault is with us: we are not fortunate in presenting the doctrines and the miracles.

But the truth is, we are not by any means so well equipped as they think. We have *not* the easy task that they imagine. To use a military figure, we are sent against the enemy with good powder in our guns, but only wads for bullets; that is to say, our miracles are not effective; the Hindoos do not care for them; they have more extraordinary ones of their own. All the details of their own religion are proven and established by miracles; the details of ours must be proven in the same way. When I first began my work in India I greatly underestimated the difficulties thus put upon my task. A correction was not long in coming. I thought as our friends think at home—that to prepare my childlike wonder-lovers to listen with favor to my grave message I only needed to charm the way to it with wonders, marvels, miracles. With full confidence I told the wonders performed by Samson, the strongest man that had ever lived—for so I called him.

At first I saw lively anticipation and strong interest in the faces of my people, but as I moved along from incident to incident of the great story, I was distressed to see that I was steadily losing the sympathy of my audience. I could not understand it. It was a surprise to me, and a disappointment. Before I was through, the fading sympathy had paled to indifference. Thence to the end the indifference remained; I was not able to make any impression upon it.

A good old Hindoo gentleman told me where my trouble lay. He said 'We Hindoos recognize a god by the work of his hands—we accept no other testimony. Apparently, this is also the rule with you Christians. And we know when a man has his power from a god by the fact that he does things which he could not do, as a man, with the mere powers of a man. Plainly, this is the Christian's way also, of knowing when a man is working by a god's power and not by his own. You saw that there was a supernatural property in the hair of Samson; for you perceived that when his hair was gone he was as other men. It is our way, as I have said. There are many nations in the world, and each group of nations has its own gods, and will pay no worship to the gods of the others. Each group believes its own gods to be strongest, and it will not exchange them except for gods that shall be proven to be their superiors in power. Man is but a weak creature, and needs the help of gods—he cannot do without it. Shall he place his fate in the hands of weak gods when there may be stronger ones to be found? That would be foolish. No, if he hear of gods that are stronger than his own, he should not turn a deaf ear, for it is not a light matter that is at stake. How then shall he determine which gods are the stronger, his own or those that preside over the concerns of other nations? By comparing the known works of his own gods with the works of those others; there is no other way. Now, when we make this comparison, we are not drawn towards the gods of any other nation. Our gods are shown by their works to be the strongest, the most powerful. The Christians have but few gods, and they are new—new, and not strong; as it seems to us. They will increase in number, it is true, for this has happened with all gods, but that time is far away, many ages and decades of ages away, for gods multiply slowly, as is meet for beings to whom a thousand years is but a single moment. Our own gods have been born millions of years apart. The process is slow, the gathering of strength and power is similarly slow. In the slow lapse of the ages the steadily accumulating power of our gods has at last become prodigious. We have a thousand proofs of this in the colossal character of their personal acts and the acts of ordinary men to whom they have given supernatural qualities. To your Samson was given supernatural power, and when he broke the withes, and slew the thousands with the jawbone of an ass, and carried away the gates of the city upon his shoulders, you were amazed—and also awed, for you recognized the divine source of his strength. But it could not profit to place these things before your Hindoo congregation and invite their wonder; for they would compare them with the deed done by Hanuman, when our gods infused their divine strength into his muscles; and they would be indifferent to them—as you saw. In the old, old times, ages and ages gone by, when our god Rama was warring with the demon god of Ceylon, Rama bethought him to bridge the sea and connect Ceylon with India, so that his armies might pass easily over; and he sent his general, Hanuman, inspired like your own Samson with divine strength, to bring the materials for the bridge. In two days Hanuman strode fifteen hundred miles, to the Himalayas, and took upon his shoulder a range of those lofty mountains two hundred miles long, and started with it toward Ceylon. It was in the night;

and, as he passed along the plain, the people of Govardhun heard the thunder of his tread and felt the earth rocking under it, and they ran out, and there, with their snowy summits piled to heaven, they saw the Himalayas passing by. And as this huge continent swept along overshadowing the earth, upon its slopes they discerned the twink-ling lights of a thousand sleeping villages, and it was as if the constellations were filing in procession through the sky. While they were looking, Hanuman stumbled, and a small ridge of red sandstone twenty miles long was jolted loose and fell. Half of its length has wasted away in the course of the ages, but the other ten miles of it remain in the plain by Govardhun to this day as proof of the might of the inspiration of our gods. You must know, yourself, that Hanuman could not have carried those mountains to Ceylon except by the strength of the gods. You know that it was not done by his own strength, therefore, you know that it was done by the strength of the gods, just as you know that Samson carried the gates by the divine strength and not by his own. I think you must concede two things: First, That in carrying the gates of the city upon his shoulders, Samson did not establish the superiority of his gods over ours; secondly, That his feat is not supported by any but verbal evidence, while Hanuman's is not only supported by verbal evidence, but this evidence is confirmed, established, proven, by visible, tangible evidence, which is the strongest of all testimony. We have the sandstone ridge, and while it remains we cannot doubt, and shall not. Have you the gates?'

5

Cecil Rhodes' Shark and His First Fortune

> The timid man yearns for full value and asks a tenth. The bold man strikes for double value and compromises on par.
>
> —*Pudd'nhead Wilson's New Calendar*

One is sure to be struck by the liberal way in which Australasia spends money upon public works—such as legislative buildings, town halls, hospitals, asylums, parks, and botanical gardens. I should say that where minor towns in America spend a hundred dollars on the town hall and on public parks and gardens, the like towns in Australasia spend a thousand. And I think that this ratio will hold good in the matter of hospitals, also. I have seen a costly and well-equipped, and architecturally handsome hospital in an Australian village of fifteen hundred inhabitants. It was built by private funds furnished by the villagers and the neighboring planters, and its running expenses were drawn from the same sources. I suppose it would be hard to match this in any country. This village was about to close a contract for lighting its streets with the electric light, when I was there. That is ahead of London. London is still obscured by gas—gas pretty widely scattered, too, in some of the districts; so widely indeed, that except on moonlight nights it is difficult to find the gas lamps.

The botanical garden of Sydney covers thirty-eight acres, beautifully laid out and rich with the spoil of all the lands and all the climes of the world. The garden is on high ground in the middle of the town, overlooking the great harbor, and it adjoins the spacious grounds of Government House—fifty-six acres; and at hand also, is a recreation ground containing eighty-two acres. In addition, there are the zoological gardens, the race-course, and the great cricket-grounds where the international matches are played. Therefore there is plenty of room for reposeful lazying and lounging, and for exercise too, for such as like that kind of work.

There are four specialties attainable in the way of social pleasure. If you enter your name on the Visitor's Book at Government House you will receive an invitation to the next ball that takes place there, if nothing can be proven against you. And it will be very pleasant; for you will see everybody except the Governor, and add a number of acquaintances and several friends to your list. The Governor will be in England. He always is. The continent has four or five governors, and I do not know how many it takes to govern the outlying archipelago; but anyway you will not see them. When they are appointed they come out from England and get inaugurated, and give a ball, and help pray for rain, and get aboard ship and go back home. And so the Lieutenant-Governor has to do all the work. I was in Australasia three months and a half, and saw only one Governor. The others were at home.

The Australasian Governor would not be so restless, perhaps, if he had a war, or a veto, or something like that to call for his reserve-energies, but he hasn't. There isn't any war, and there isn't any veto in his hands. And so there is really little or nothing doing in his line. The country governs itself, and prefers to do it; and is so strenuous about it and so jealous of its independence that it grows restive if even the Imperial Government at home proposes to help; and so the Imperial veto, while a fact, is yet mainly a name.

Thus the Governor's functions are much more limited than are a Governor's functions with us. And therefore more fatiguing. He is the apparent head of the State, he is the real head of Society. He represents culture, refinement, elevated sentiment, polite life, religion; and by his example he propagates these, and they spread and flourish and bear good fruit. He creates the fashion, and leads it. His ball is the ball of balls, and his countenance makes the horse-race thrive.

He is usually a lord, and this is well; for his position compels him to lead an expensive life, and an English lord is generally well equipped for that.

Another of Sydney's social pleasures is the visit to the Admiralty House; which is nobly situated on high ground overlooking the water. The trim boats of the service convey the guests thither; and there, or on board the flag-ship, they have the duplicate of the hospitalities of Government House. The Admiral commanding a station in British waters is a magnate of the first degree, and he is sumptuously housed, as becomes the dignity of his office.

Third in the list of special pleasures is the tour of the harbor in a fine steam pleasure-launch. Your richer friends own boats of this kind, and they will invite you, and the joys of the trip will make a long day seem short.

And finally comes the shark-fishing. Sydney Harbor is populous with the finest breeds of man-eating sharks in the world. Some people make their living catching them; for the Government pays a cash bounty on them. The larger the shark the larger the bounty, and some of the sharks are twenty feet long. You not only get the bounty, but everything that is in the shark belongs to you. Sometimes the contents are quite valuable.

The shark is the swiftest fish that swims. The speed of the fastest steamer afloat is poor compared to his. And he is a great gad-about, and roams far and wide in the oceans, and visits the shores of all of them, ultimately, in the course of his restless excursions. I have a tale to tell now, which has not as yet been in print. In 1870 a young stranger arrived in Sydney, and set about finding something to do; but he knew no one, and brought no recommendations, and the result was that he got no employment. He had aimed high, at first, but as time and his money wasted away he grew less and less exacting, until at last he was willing to serve in the humblest capacities if so he might get bread and shelter. But luck was still against him; he could find no opening of any sort. Finally his money was all gone. He walked the streets all day, thinking; he walked them all night, thinking, thinking, and growing hungrier and hungrier. At dawn he found himself well away from the town and drifting aimlessly along the harbor shore. As he was passing by a nodding shark-fisher the man looked up and said—

>'Say, young fellow, take my line a spell, and change my luck for me.'
>
>'How do you know I won't make it worse?'
>
>'Because you can't. It has been at its worst all night. If you can't change it, no harm's done; if you do change it, it's for the better, of course. Come.'
>
>'All right, what will you give?'
>
>'I'll give you the shark, if you catch one.'
>
>'And I will eat it, bones and all. Give me the line.'
>
>'Here you are. I will get away, now, for awhile, so that my luck won't spoil yours; for many and many a time I've noticed that if—there, pull in, pull in, man, you've got a bite! I knew how it would be. Why, I knew you for a born son of luck the minute I saw you. All right—he's landed.'

It was an unusually large shark—'a full nineteen-footer,' the fisherman said, as he laid the creature open with his knife.

>'Now you rob him, young man, while I step to my hamper for a fresh bait. There's generally

something in them worth going for. You've changed my luck, you see. But my goodness, I hope you haven't changed your own.'

'Oh, it wouldn't matter; don't worry about that. Get your bait. I'll rob him.'

When the fisherman got back the young man had just finished washing his hands in the bay, and was starting away.

'What, you are not going?'

'Yes. Good-bye.'

'But what about your shark?'

'The shark? Why, what use is he to me?'

'What *use* is he? I like that. Don't you know that we can go and report him to Government, and you'll get a clean solid eighty shillings bounty? Hard cash, you know. What do you think about it now?'

'Oh, well, you can collect it.'

'And *keep* it? Is that what you mean?'

'Yes.'

'Well, this is odd. You're one of those sort they call eccentrics, I judge. The saying is, you mustn't judge a man by his clothes, and I'm believing it now. Why yours are looking just ratty, don't you know; and yet you must be rich.'

'I am.'

The young man walked slowly back to the town, deeply musing as he went. He halted a moment in front of the best restaurant, then glanced at his clothes and passed on, and got his breakfast at a 'stand-up.' There was a good deal of it, and it cost five shillings.

He tendered a sovereign, got his change, glanced at his silver, muttered to himself, 'There isn't enough to buy clothes with' and went his way.

At half-past nine the richest wool-broker in Sydney was sitting in his morning-room at home, settling his breakfast with the morning paper. A servant put his head in and said:

> 'There's a sundowner at the door wants to see you, sir.'
>
> 'What do you bring that kind of a message here for? Send him about his business.'
>
> 'He won't go, sir. I've tried.'
>
> 'He won't go? That's—why, that's unusual. He's one of two things, then: he's a remarkable person, or he's crazy. Is he crazy?'
>
> 'No, sir. He don't look it.'
>
> 'Then he's remarkable. What does he say he wants?'
>
> 'He won't tell, sir; only says it's very important.'
>
> 'And won't go. Does he *say* he won't go?'
>
> 'Says he'll stand there till he sees you, sir, if it's all day.'
>
> 'And yet isn't crazy. Show him up.'

The sundowner was shown in. The broker said to himself, 'No, he's not crazy; that is easy to see; so he must be the other thing.' Then aloud,

> 'Well, my good fellow, be quick about it; don't waste any words; what is it you want?'
>
> 'I want to borrow a hundred thousand pounds.'

'Scott! (It's a mistake; he *is* crazy... No—he *can't* be—not with that eye.) Why, you take my breath away. Come, who *are* you?'

'Nobody that you know.'

'What is your name?'

'Cecil Rhodes.'

'No, I don't remember hearing the name before. Now then—just for curiosity's sake—what has sent you to me on this extraordinary errand?'

'The intention to make a hundred thousand pounds for you and as much for myself within the next sixty days.'

'Well, well, well. It is the most extraordinary idea that I—sit *down*—you interest me. And somehow you—well, you fascinate me; I think that that is about the word. And it isn't your proposition—no, that doesn't fascinate me; it's something else, I don't quite know what; something that's born in you and oozes out of you, I suppose. Now then—just for curiosity's sake again, nothing more: as I understand it, it is your desire to bor—'

'I said *intention*.'

'Pardon, so you did. I thought it was an unheedful use of the word—an unheedful valuing of its strength, you know.'

'I knew its strength.'

'Well, I must say—but look here, let me walk the floor a little, my mind is getting into a sort of whirl, though *you* don't seem disturbed any. (Plainly this young fellow isn't crazy; but as to his being remarkable—well, really he amounts to that, and something over.) Now then, I believe I am beyond the reach of further astonishment. Strike, and spare not. What is your scheme?'

'To buy the wool crop—deliverable in sixty days.'

'What, the *whole* of it?'

'The whole of it.'

'No, I was not quite out of the reach of surprises, after all. Why, how you talk! Do you know what our crop is going to foot up?'

'Two and a half million sterling—maybe a little more.'

'Well, you've got your statistics right, any way. Now, then, do you know what the margins would foot up, to buy it at sixty days?'

'The hundred thousand pounds I came here to get.'

'Right, once more. Well, dear me, just to see what would happen, I wish you had the money. And if you had it, what would you do with it?'

'I shall make two hundred thousand pounds out of it in sixty days.'

'You mean, of course, that you *might* make it if—'

'I said "shall".'

'Yes, by George, you *did* say "shall"! You are the most definite devil I ever saw, in the matter of language. Dear, dear, dear, look here! Definite speech means clarity of mind. Upon my word I believe you've got what you believe to be a rational *reason* for venturing into this house, an entire stranger, on this wild scheme of buying the wool crop of an entire colony on speculation. Bring it out—I am prepared—acclimatized, if I may use the word. *Why* would you buy the crop, and *why* would you make that sum out of it? That is to say, what makes you think you—'

'I don't think—I know.'

'Definite again. *How* do you know?'

'Because France has declared war against Germany, and wool has gone up fourteen per cent in London and is still rising.'

'Oh, in-deed? Now then, I've *got* you! Such a thunderbolt as you have just let fly ought to have made me jump out of my chair, but it didn't stir me the least little bit, you see. And for a very simple reason: I have read the morning paper. You can look at it if you want to. The fastest ship in the service arrived at eleven o'clock last night, fifty days out from London. All her news is printed here. There are no war-clouds anywhere; and as for wool, why, it is the low-spiritedest commodity in the English market. It is your turn to jump, now... Well, why, don't you jump? Why do you sit there in that placid fashion, when—'

'Because I have later news.'

'Later news? Oh, come—later news than fifty days, brought steaming hot from London by the—'

'My news is only ten days old.'

'Oh, Mun-*chausen*, hear the maniac talk! Where did you get it?'

'Got it out of a shark.'

'Oh, oh, oh, this is *too* much! Front! call the police—bring the gun—raise the town! All the asylums in Christendom have broken loose in the single person of—'

'Sit down! And collect yourself. Where is the use in getting excited? Am I excited? There is nothing to get excited *about*. When I make a statement which I cannot prove, it will be time enough for you to begin to offer hospitality to damaging fancies about me and my sanity.'

'Oh, a thousand, thousand pardons! I ought to be ashamed of myself, and I *am* ashamed of myself for thinking that a little bit of a circumstance like sending a shark to England to fetch back a market report—'

'What does your middle initial stand for, sir?'

'Andrew. What are you writing?'

'Wait a moment. Proof about the shark—and another matter. Only ten lines. There—now it is done. Sign it.'

'Many thanks—many. Let me see; it says—it says—oh, come, this is *interesting!* Why—why—look here! Prove what you say here, and I'll put up the money, and double as much, if necessary, and divide the winnings with you, half and half. There, now—I've signed; make your promise good if you can. Show me a copy of the London *Times* only ten days old.'

'Here it is—and with it these buttons and a memorandum book that belonged to the man the shark swallowed. Swallowed him in the Thames, without a doubt; for you will notice that the last entry in the book is dated "London", and is of the same date as the *Times*, and says, "Der confequents der Kreigeseflarun, reise ich heute nach Deutchland ab, aur bak ich mein leben auf dem Ultar meines Landes legen mag"—, as clean native German as anybody can put upon paper, and means that in consequence of the declaration of war, this loyal soul is leaving for home *to-day*, to fight. And he did leave, too, but the shark had him before the day was done, poor fellow.'

'And a pity, too. But there are times for mourning, and we will attend to this case further on; other matters are pressing, now. I will go down and set the machinery in motion in a quiet way and buy the crop. It will cheer the drooping spirits of the boys, in a transitory way. Everything is transitory in this world. Sixty days hence, when they are called to deliver the goods, they will think they've been struck by lightning. But there is a time for mourning, and we will attend to that case along with the other one. Come along, I'll take you to my tailor. What did you say your name is?'

'Cecil Rhodes.'

'It is hard to remember. However, I think you will make it easier by and by, if you live. There are three kinds of people—Commonplace Men, Remarkable Men, and Lunatics. I'll classify you with the Remarkables, and take the chances.'

The deal went through, and secured to the young stranger the first fortune he ever pocketed.

The people of Sydney ought to be afraid of the sharks, but for some reason they do not seem to be. On Saturdays the young men go out in their boats, and sometimes the water is fairly covered with the little sails. A boat upsets now and then, by accident, a result of tumultuous skylarking; sometimes the boys upset their boat for fun—such as it is—with sharks visibly waiting around for just such an occurrence. The young fellows scramble aboard whole—sometimes—not always. Tragedies have happened more than once. While I was in Sydney it was reported that a boy fell out of a boat in the mouth of the Paramatta river and screamed for help and a boy jumped overboard from another boat to save him from the assembling sharks; but the sharks made swift work with the lives of both.

The government pays a bounty for the shark; to get the bounty the fishermen bait the hook or the seine with agreeable mutton; the news spreads and the sharks come from all over the Pacific Ocean to get the free board. In time the shark culture will be one of the most successful things in the colony.

6

Bad Health—To Melbourne

> We can secure other people's approval,
> if we do right and try hard; but our own
> is worth a hundred of it, and no way
> has been found out of securing that.
>
> —*Pudd'nhead Wilson's New Calendar*

My health had broken down in New York in May; it had remained in a doubtful but fairish condition during a succeeding period of 82 days; it broke again on the Pacific. It broke again in Sydney, but not until after I had had a good outing, and had also filled my lecture engagements. This latest break lost me the chance of seeing Queensland. In the circumstances, to go north toward hotter weather was not advisable.

So we moved south with a westward slant, 17 hours by rail to the capital of the colony of Victoria, Melbourne—that juvenile city of sixty years, and half a million inhabitants. On the map the distance looked small; but that is a trouble with all divisions of distance in such a vast country as Australia. The colony of Victoria itself looks small on the map—looks like a county, in fact—yet it is about as large as England, Scotland, and Wales combined. Or, to get another focus upon it, it is just 80 times as large as the state of Rhode Island, and one-third as large as the State of Texas.

Outside of Melbourne, Victoria seems to be owned by a handful of squatters, each with a Rhode Island for a sheep farm. That is the impression which one gathers from common talk, yet the wool industry of Victoria is by no means so great as that of New South Wales. The climate of Victoria is favorable to other great industries—among others, wheat-growing and the making of wine.

We took the train at Sydney at about four in the afternoon. It was American in one way, for we had a most rational sleeping car; also the car was clean and fine and new—nothing about it to suggest the rolling stock of the continent of Europe. But our baggage was weighed, and extra weight charged for. That was continental. Continental and troublesome. Any detail of railroading that is not troublesome cannot honorably be described as continental.

The tickets were round-trip ones—to Melbourne, and clear to Adelaide in South Australia, and then all the way back to Sydney. Twelve hundred more miles than we really expected to make; but then as the round trip wouldn't cost much more than the single trip, it seemed well enough to buy as many miles as one could afford, even if one was not likely to need them.

A human being has a natural desire to have more of a good thing than he needs.

Now comes a singular thing: the oddest thing, the strangest thing, the most baffling and unaccountable marvel that Australasia can show. At the frontier between New South Wales and Victoria our multitude of passengers were routed out of their snug beds by lantern-light in the morning in the biting cold of a high altitude to change cars on a road that has no break in it from Sydney to Melbourne! Think of the paralysis of intellect that gave that idea birth; imagine the boulder it emerged from on some petrified legislator's shoulders.

It is a narrow-gauge road to the frontier, and a broader gauge thence to Melbourne. The two governments were the builders of the road and are the owners of it. One or two reasons are given for this curious state of things. One is, that it represents the jealousy existing between the colonies—the two most important colonies of Australasia. What the other one is, I have forgotten. But it is of no consequence. It could be but another effort to explain the inexplicable.

All passengers fret at the double-gauge; all shippers of freight must of course fret at it; unnecessary expense, delay, and annoyance are imposed upon everybody concerned, and no one is benefited.

Each Australian colony fences itself off from its neighbor with a customhouse. Personally, I have no objection, but it must be a good deal of inconvenience to the people. We have something resembling it here and there in America, but it goes by another name. The large empire of the Pacific coast requires a world of iron machinery, and could manufacture it economically on the spot if the imposts on foreign iron were removed. But they are not. Protection to Pennsylvania and Alabama forbids it. The result to the Pacific coast is the same as if there were several rows of customfences between the coast and the East. Iron carted across the American continent at luxurious railway rates would be valuable enough to be coined when it arrived.

We changed cars. This was at Albury. And it was there, I think, that the growing day and the early sun exposed the distant range called the Blue Mountains. Accurately named. 'My word!' as the Australians say, but it was a stunning color, that blue. Deep, strong, rich, exquisite; towering and majestic masses of blue—a softly luminous blue, a smouldering blue, as if vaguely lit by fires within. It extinguished the blue of the sky—made it pallid and unwholesome, whitey and washed-out. A wonderful color—just divine.

A resident told me that those were not mountains; he said they were rabbit-piles. And explained that long exposure and the over-ripe condition of the rabbits was what made them look so blue. This man may have been right, but much reading of books of travel has made me distrustful of gratis information furnished by unofficial residents of a country. The facts which such people give to travelers are usually erroneous, and often intemperately so. The rabbit-plague has indeed been very bad in Australia, and it could account for one mountain, but not for a mountain range, it seems to me. It is too large an order.

We breakfasted at the station. A good breakfast, except the coffee; and cheap. The Government establishes the prices and placards them. The waiters were men, I think; but that is not usual in Australasia. The usual thing is to have girls. No, not girls, young ladies—generally duchesses. Dress? They would attract attention at any royal levée in Europe. Even empresses and queens do not dress as they do. Not that they could not afford it, perhaps, but they would not know how.

All the pleasant morning we slid smoothly along over the plains, through thin—not thick—forests of great melancholy gum trees, with trunks rugged with curled sheets of flaking bark—erysipelas convalescents, so to speak, shedding their dead skins. And all along were tiny cabins, built sometimes of wood, sometimes of gray-blue corrugated iron; and the doorsteps and fences were clogged with children—rugged little simply-clad chaps that looked as if they had been imported from the banks of the Mississippi without breaking bulk.

And there were little villages, with neat stations well placarded with showy advertisements—mainly of almost *too* self-righteous brands of 'sheep-dip.' If that is the name—and I think it is. It is a stuff like tar, and is dabbed on to places where the shearer clips a piece out of the sheep. It bars out the flies, and has healing properties, and a nip to it which makes the sheep skip like the cattle on a thousand hills. It is not good to eat. That is, it is not good to eat except when mixed with railroad coffee. It improves railroad coffee. Without it railroad coffee is too vague. But with it, it is quite assertive and enthusiastic. By itself, railroad coffee is too passive; but sheep-dip makes it wake up and get down to business. I wonder where they get railroad coffee?

We saw birds, but not a kangaroo, not an emu, not an ornithorhyncus, not a lecturer, not a native. Indeed, the land seemed quite destitute of game. But I have misused the word native. In Australia it is applied to Australian-born whites only. I should have said that we saw no Aboriginals—no 'blackfellows.' And to this day I have never seen one. In the great museums you will find all the other curiosities, but in the curio of chiefest interest to the stranger all of them are lacking. We have at home an abundance of museums, and not an American Indian in them. It is clearly an absurdity, but it never struck me before.

7

Wagga-Wagga—The Tichborne Claimant

> Truth is stranger than fiction—
> to some people, but I am measurably
> familiar with it.
>
> —*Pudd'nhead Wilson's New Calendar*

> Truth is stranger than fiction, but it
> is because Fiction is obliged to
> stick to possibilities; Truth isn't.
>
> —*Pudd'nhead Wilson's New Calendar*

The air was balmy and delicious, the sunshine radiant; it was a charming excursion. In the course of it we came to a town whose odd name was famous all over the world a quarter of a century ago—Wagga-Wagga. This was because the Tichborne Claimant had kept a butcher-shop there. It was out of the midst of his humble collection of sausages and tripe that he soared up into the zenith of notoriety and hung there in the wastes of space and time, with the telescopes of all nations leveled at him in unappeasable curiosity—curiosity as to which of the two long-missing persons he was: Arthur Orton, the mislaid roustabout of Wapping, or Sir Roger Tichborne, the lost heir of a name and estates as old as English history. We all know now, but not a dozen people knew then; and the dozen kept the mystery to themselves and allowed the most intricate and fascinating and marvelous real-life romance that has ever been played upon the world's stage to unfold itself serenely, act by act, in a British court by the long and laborious processes of judicial development.

When we recall the details of that great romance we marvel to see what daring chances truth may freely take in constructing a tale, as compared with the poor little conservative risks permitted to fiction. The fiction-artist could achieve no success with the materials of this splendid Tichborne romance.

He would have to drop out the chief characters; the public would say such people are impossible. He would have to drop out a number of the most picturesque incidents; the public would say such things could never happen. And yet the chief characters did exist, and the incidents did happen.

It cost the Tichborne estates $400,000 to unmask the Claimant and drive him out; and even after the exposure multitudes of Englishmen still believed in him. It cost the British Government another $400,000 to convict him of perjury; and after the conviction the same old multitudes still believed in him; and among these believers were many educated and intelligent men; and some of them had personally known the real Sir Roger. The Claimant was sentenced to 14 years' imprisonment. When he got out of prison he went to New York and kept a whisky saloon in the Bowery for a time, then disappeared from view.

He always claimed to be Sir Roger Tichborne until death called for him. This was but a few months ago—not very much short of a generation since he left Wagga-Wagga to go and possess himself of his estates. On his death-bed he yielded up his secret, and confessed in writing that he was only Arthur Orton of Wapping, able seaman and butcher—that and nothing more. But it is scarcely to be doubted that there are people whom even his dying confession will not convince. The old habit of assimilating incredibilities must have made strong food a necessity in their case; a weaker article would probably disagree with them.

I was in London when the Claimant stood his trial for perjury. I attended one of his showy evenings in the sumptuous quarters provided for him from the purses of his adherents and well-wishers. He was in evening dress, and I thought him a rather fine and stately creature. There were about twenty-five gentlemen present; educated men, men moving in good society, none of them commonplace; some of them were men of distinction, none of them were obscurities. They were his cordial friends and admirers. It was 'S'r Roger,' always 'S'r Roger,' on all hands; no one withheld the title, all turned it from the tongue with unction, and as if it tasted good.

For many years I had had a mystery in stock. Melbourne, and only Melbourne, could unriddle it for me. In 1873 I arrived in London with my wife and young child, and presently received a note from Naples signed by a name not familiar to me. It was not Bascom, and it was not Henry; but I will call it Henry Bascom for convenience's sake. This note, of about six lines, was written on a strip of white paper whose end-edges were ragged. I came to be familiar with those strips in later years. Their size and pattern were always the same. Their contents were usually to the same effect: would I and mine come to the writer's country-place in England on such and such a date, by such and such a train, and stay twelve days and depart by such and such a train at the end of the specified time? A carriage would meet us at the station.

These invitations were always for a long time ahead; if we were in Europe, three months ahead; if we were in America, six to twelve months ahead. They always named the exact date and train for the beginning and also for the end of the visit.

This first note invited us for a date three months in the future. It asked us to arrive by the 4.10 p.m. train from London, August 6th. The carriage would be waiting. The carriage would take us away seven days later—train specified. And there were these words: 'Speak to Tom Hughes.'

I showed the note to the author of 'Tom Brown at Rugby,' and he said—

'Accept, and be thankful.'

He described Mr. Bascom as being a man of genius, a man of fine attainments, a choice man in every way, a rare and beautiful character. He said that Bascom Hall was a particularly fine example of the stately manorial mansion of Elizabeth's days, and that it was a house worth going a long way to see—like Knowle; that Mr. B. was of a social disposition, liked the company of agreeable people, and always had samples of the sort coming and going.

We paid the visit. We paid others, in later years—the last one in 1879. Soon after that Mr. Bascom started on a voyage around the world in a steam yacht—a long and leisurely trip, for he was making collections, in all lands, of birds, butterflies, and such things.

The day that President Garfield was shot by the assassin Guiteau, we were at a little watering place on Long Island Sound; and in the mail matter of that day came a letter with the Melbourne post-mark on it. It was for my wife, but I recognized Mr. Bascom's handwriting on the envelope, and opened it. It was the usual note—as to paucity of lines—and was written on the customary strip of paper, but there was nothing usual about the contents. The note informed my wife that if it would be any assuagement of her grief to know that her husband's lecture-tour in Australia was a satisfactory venture from the beginning to the end, he, the writer, could testify that such was the case; also, that her husband's untimely death had been mourned by all classes, as she would already know by the press telegrams, long before the reception of this note; that the funeral was attended by the officials of the colonial and city governments; and that while he, the writer, her friend and mine, had not reached Melbourne in time to see the body, he had at least had the sad privilege of acting as one of the pall-bearers. Signed, 'Henry Bascom.'

My first thought was, why didn't he have the coffin opened? He would have seen that the corpse was an imposter, and he could have gone right ahead and dried up the most of those tears, and comforted those sorrowing governments, and sold the remains and sent me the money.

I did nothing about the matter. I had set the law after living lecture-doubles of mine a couple of times in America, and the law had not been able to catch them; others in my trade had tried to catch *their* impostor-doubles and had failed. Then where was the use in harrying a ghost? None—and so I did not disturb it. I had a curiosity to know about that man's lecture-tour and last moments, but that could wait. When I should see Mr. Bascom he would tell me all about it. But he passed from life, and I never saw him again. My curiosity faded away.

However, when I found that I was going to Australia it revived. And naturally: for if the people should say that I was a dull, poor thing compared to what I was before I died, it would have a bad effect on business. Well, to my surprise the Sydney journalists had *never heard of that impostor*! I pressed them, but they were firm—they had never heard of him, and didn't believe in him.

I could not understand it; still, I thought it would all come right in Melbourne. The government would remember; and the other mourners. At the supper of the Institute of Journalists I should find out all about the matter. But no—it turned out that *they* had never heard of it.

So my mystery was a mystery still. It was a great disappointment. I believed it would never be cleared up—in this life—so I dropped it out of my mind.

But at last! Just when I was least expecting it—

However, this is not the place for the rest of it; I shall come to the matter again, in a far-distant chapter.

8

The Australian Larrikin—Is He Dead?

> There is a Moral sense, and there is an Immoral Sense. History shows us that the Moral Sense enables us to perceive morality and how to avoid it, and that the Immoral Sense enables us to perceive immorality and how to enjoy it.
>
> —*Pudd'nhead Wilson's New Calendar*

Melbourne spreads around over an immense area of ground. It is a stately city architecturally as well as in magnitude. It has an elaborate system of cable-car service; it has museums, and colleges, and schools, and public gardens, and electricity, and gas, and libraries, and theaters, and mining centers, and wool centers, and centers of the arts and sciences, and boards of trade, and ships, and railroads, and a harbor, and social clubs, and journalistic clubs, and racing clubs, and a squatter club sumptuously housed and appointed, and as many churches and banks as can make a living. In a word, it is equipped with everything that goes to make the modern great city. It is the largest city of Australasia, and fills the post with honor and credit. It has one specialty; this must not be jumbled in with those other things. It is the mitred Metropolitan of the Horse-Racing Cult. Its raceground is the Mecca of Australasia. On the great annual day of sacrifice—the 5th of November, Guy Fawkes's Day—business is suspended over a stretch of land and sea as wide as from New York to San Francisco, and deeper than from the northern lakes to the Gulf of Mexico; and every man and woman, of high degree or low, who can afford the expense, put away their other duties and come. They begin to swarm in by ship and rail a fortnight before the day, and they swarm thicker and thicker day after day, until all the vehicles of transportation are taxed to their uttermost to meet the demands of the occasion, and all hotels and lodgings are bulging outward because of the pressure from within. They come a hundred thousand strong, as all the best authorities say, and they pack the spacious grounds and grand-stands and make a spectacle such as is never to be seen in Australasia elsewhere.

It is the 'Melbourne Cup' that brings this multitude together. Their clothes have been ordered long ago, at unlimited cost, and without bounds as to beauty and magnificence, and have been kept in concealment until now, for unto this day are they consecrate. I am speaking of the *ladies*' clothes; but one might know that.

And so the grand-stands make a brilliant and wonderful spectacle, a delirium of color, a vision of beauty.

The champagne flows, everybody is vivacious, excited, happy; everybody bets, and gloves and fortunes change hands right along, all the time. Day after day the races go on, and the fun and the excitement are kept at white heat; and when each day is done, the people dance all night so as to be fresh for the race in the morning. And at the end of the great week the swarms secure lodgings and transportation for next year, then flock away to their remote homes and count their gains and losses, and order next year's Cup-clothes, and then lie down and sleep two weeks, and get up sorry to reflect that a whole year must be put in somehow or other before they can be wholly happy again.

The Melbourne Cup is the Australasian National Day. It would be difficult to overstate its importance. It overshadows all other holidays and specialized days of whatever sort in that congeries of colonies. Overshadows them? I might almost say it blots them out. Each of them gets attention, but not everybody's; each of them evokes interest, but not everybody's; each of them rouses enthusiasm, but not everybody's; in each case a part of the attention, interest, and enthusiasm is a matter of habit and custom, and another part of it is official and perfunctory. Cup Day, and Cup Day only, commands an attention, an interest, and an enthusiasm which are universal—and spontaneous, not perfunctory. Cup Day is supreme—it has no rival. I can call to mind no specialized annual day, in any country, which can be named by that large name—Supreme. I can call to mind no specialized annual day, in any country, whose approach fires the whole land with a conflagration of conversation and preparation and anticipation and jubilation. No day save this one; but this one does it.

In America we have no annual supreme day; no day whose approach makes the whole nation glad. We have the Fourth of July, and Christmas, and Thanksgiving. Neither of them can claim the primacy; neither of them can arouse an enthusiasm which comes near to being universal. Eight grown Americans out of ten dread the coming of the Fourth, with its pandemonium and its perils, and they rejoice when it is gone—if still alive. The approach of Christmas brings harassment and dread to many excellent people. They have to buy a cartload of presents, and they never know what to buy to hit the various tastes; they put in three weeks of hard and anxious work, and when Christmas morning comes they are so dissatisfied with the result, and so disappointed that they want to sit down and cry. Then they give thanks that Christmas comes but once a year. The observance of Thanksgiving Day—as a function—has become general of late years. The Thankfulness is not so general. This is natural. Two-thirds of the nation have always had hard luck and a hard time during the year, and this has a calming effect upon their enthusiasm.

We *have* a supreme day—a sweeping and tremendous and tumultuous day, a day which commands an absolute universality of interest and excitement; but it is not annual. It comes but once in four years; therefore it cannot count as a rival of the Melbourne Cup.

In Great Britain and Ireland they have two great days—Christmas and the Queen's birthday. But they are equally popular; there is no supremacy.

I think it must be conceded that the position of the Australasian Day is unique, solitary, unfellowed; and likely to hold that high place a long time.

The next things which interest us when we travel are, first, the people; next, the novelties; and finally the history of the places and countries visited. Novelties are rare in cities which represent the most advanced civilization of the modern day. When one is familiar with such cities in the other parts of the world he is in effect familiar with the cities of Australasia. The outside aspects will furnish little that is new. There will be new names, but the things which they represent will sometimes be found to be less new than their names. There may be shades of difference, but these can easily be too fine for detection by the incompetent eye of the passing stranger. In the larrikin he will not be able to discover a new species, but only an old one met elsewhere, and variously called loafer, rough, tough, bummer, or blatherskite, according to his geographical distribution. The larrikin differs by a shade from those others, in that he is more sociable toward the stranger than they, more kindly disposed, more hospitable, more hearty, more friendly. At least it seemed so to me, and I had opportunity to observe. In Sydney, at least. In Melbourne I had to drive to and from the lecture-theater, but in Sydney I was able to walk both ways, and did it. Every night, on my way home at ten, or a quarter past, I found the larrikin grouped in considerable force at several of the street corners, and he always gave me this pleasant salutation:

'Hello, Mark!'
'Here's to you, old chap!'

'Say—Mark!—is he dead?'—a reference to a passage in some book of mine, though I did not detect, at that time, that that was its source. And I didn't detect it afterward in Melbourne, when I came on the stage for the first time, and the same question was dropped down upon me from the dizzy height of the gallery. It is always difficult to answer a sudden inquiry like that, when you have come unprepared and don't know what it means. I will remark here—if it is not an indecorum—that the welcome which an American lecturer gets from a British colonial audience is a thing which will move him to his deepest deeps, and veil his sight and break his voice. And from Winnipeg to Africa, experience will teach him nothing; he will never learn to expect it, it will catch him as a surprise each time. The war-cloud hanging black over England and America made no trouble for me. I was a prospective prisoner of war, but at dinners, suppers, on the platform, and elsewhere, there was never anything to remind me of it. This was hospitality of the right metal, and would have been prominently lacking in some countries, in the circumstances.

And speaking of the war-flurry, it seemed to me to bring to light the unexpected, in a detail or two. It seemed to relegate the war-talk to the politicians on both sides of the water; whereas whenever a prospective war between two nations had been in the air theretofore, the public had done most of the talking and the bitterest. The attitude of the newspapers was new also. I speak of those of Australasia and India, for I had access to those only. They treated the subject argumentatively and with dignity, not with spite and anger. That was a new spirit, too, and not learned of the French and German press, either before Sedan or since. I heard many public speeches, and they reflected the moderation of the journals. The outlook is that the English-speaking race will dominate the earth a hundred years from now, if its sections do not get to fighting each other. It would be a pity to spoil that prospect by baffling and retarding wars when arbitration would settle their differences so much better and also so much more definitely.

No, as I have suggested, novelties are rare in the great capitals of modern times. Even the wool exchange in Melbourne could not be told from the familiar stock exchange of other countries. Wool brokers are just like stock-brokers; they all bounce from their seats and put up their hands and yell in unison—no stranger can tell what—and the president calmly says 'Sold to Smith & Co., threppence farthing—next!'—when probably nothing of the kind happened; for how should he know?

In the museums you will find acres of the most strange and fascinating things; but all museums are fascinating, and they do so tire your eyes, and break your back, and burn out your vitalities with their consuming interest. You always say you will never go again, but you do go. The palaces of the rich, in Melbourne, are much like the palaces of the rich in America, and the life in them is the same; but there the resemblance ends. The grounds surrounding the American palace are not often large, and not often beautiful, but in the Melbourne case the grounds are often ducally spacious, and the climate and the gardeners together make them as beautiful as a dream. It is said that some of the country seats have grounds—domains—about them which rival in charm and magnitude those which surround the country mansion of an English lord; but I was not out in the country; I had my hands full in town.

And what was the origin of this majestic city and its efflorescence of palatial town houses and country seats? Its first brick was laid and its first house built by a passing convict. Australian history is almost always picturesque; indeed, it is so curious and strange, that it is itself the chiefest novelty the country has to offer, and so it pushes the other novelties into second and third place. It does not read like history, but like the most beautiful lies. And all of a fresh new sort, no mouldy old stale ones. It is full of surprises, and adventures, and incongruities, and contradictions, and incredibilities; but they are all true, they all happened.

9

To Adelaide

> The English are mentioned in the Bible:
> Blessed are the meek, for they shall
> inherit the earth.
>
> —*Pudd'nhead Wilson's New Calendar*

When we consider the immensity of the British Empire in territory, population, and trade, it requires a stern exercise of faith to believe in the figures which represent Australasia's contribution to the Empire's commercial grandeur. As compared with the landed estate of the British Empire, the landed estate dominated by any other Power except one—Russia—is not very impressive for size. My authorities make the British Empire not much short of a fourth larger than the Russian Empire. Roughly proportioned, if you will allow your entire hand to represent the British Empire, you may then cut off the fingers a trifle above the middle joint of the middle finger, and what is left of the hand will represent Russia. The populations ruled by Great Britain and China are about the same—400,000,000 each. No other Power approaches these figures. Even Russia is left far behind.

The population of Australasia—4,000,000—sinks into nothingness, and is lost from sight in that British ocean of 400,000,000. Yet the statistics indicate that it rises again and shows up very conspicuously when its share of the Empire's commerce is the matter under consideration. The value of England's annual exports and imports is stated at three billions of dollars, and it is claimed that more than one-tenth of this great aggregate is represented by Australasia's exports to England and imports from England.[1] In addition to this, Australasia does a trade with countries other than England, amounting to a hundred million dollars a year, and a domestic inter-colonial trade amounting to a hundred and fifty millions.[2]

In round numbers the 4,000,000 buy and sell about $600,000,000 worth of goods a year. It is claimed that about half of this represents commodities of Australasian production. The products exported annually by India are worth a trifle over $500,000,000. Now, here are some faith-straining figures:

Indian production (300,000,000 population), $500,000,000.
Australasian production (4,000,000 population), $300,000,000.

That is to say, the product of the individual Indian, annually (for export some whither), is worth $1.75;

that of the individual Australasian (for export some whither), $75! Or, to put it in another way, the Indian family of man and wife and three children sends away an annual result worth $8.75, while the Australasian family sends away $375 worth.

There are trustworthy statistics furnished by Sir Richard Temple and others, which show that the individual Indian's whole annual product, both for export and home use, is worth in gold only $7.50; or, $37.50 for the family-aggregate. Ciphered out on a like ratio of multiplication, the Australasian family's aggregate production would be nearly $1,600. Truly, nothing is so astonishing as figures, if they once get started.

We left Melbourne by rail for Adelaide, the capital of the vast Province of South Australia—a seventeen-hour excursion. On the train we found several Sydney friends; among them a Judge who was going out on circuit, and was going to hold court at Broken Hill, where the celebrated silver mine is. It seemed a curious road to take to get to that region. Broken Hill is close to the western border of New South Wales, and Sydney is on the eastern border. A fairly straight line, 700 miles long, drawn westward from Sydney, would strike Broken Hill, just as a somewhat shorter one drawn west from Boston would strike Buffalo. The way the Judge was traveling would carry him over 2,000 miles by rail, he said; southwest from Sydney down to Melbourne, then northward up to Adelaide, then a cant back northeastward and over the border into New South Wales once more—to Broken Hill. It was like going from Boston southwest to Richmond, Virginia, then northwest up to Erie, Pennsylvania, then a cant back northeast and over the border—to Buffalo, New York.

But the explanation was simple. Years ago the fabulously rich silver discovery at Broken Hill burst suddenly upon an unexpected world. Its stocks started at shillings, and went by leaps and bounds to the most fanciful figures. It was one of those cases where the cook puts a month's wages into shares, and comes next month and buys your house at your own price, and moves into it herself; where the coachman takes a few shares, and next month sets up a bank; and where the common sailor invests the price of a spree, and next month buys out the steamship company and goes into business on his own hook. In a word, it was one of those excitements which bring multitudes of people to a common center with a rush, and whose needs must be supplied, and at once. Adelaide was close by, Sydney was far away. Adelaide threw a short railway across the border before Sydney had time to arrange for a long one; it was not worth while for Sydney to arrange at all. The whole vast trade-profit of Broken Hill fell into Adelaide's hands, irrevocably. New South Wales furnishes law for Broken Hill and sends her Judges 2,000 miles—mainly through alien countries—to administer it, but Adelaide takes the dividends and makes no moan.

We started at 4.20 in the afternoon, and moved across level plains until night. In the morning we had a stretch of 'scrub' country—the kind of thing which is so useful to the Australian novelist. In the scrub the hostile aboriginal lurks, and flits mysteriously about, slipping out from time to time to surprise and slaughter the settler; then slipping back again, and leaving no track that the white man can follow. In the scrub the novelist's heroine gets lost, search fails of result; she wanders here and there, and finally sinks down exhausted and unconscious, and the searchers pass within a yard or two of her, not suspecting that she is near, and by and by some rambler finds her bones and the pathetic diary which she had scribbled with her failing hand and left behind. Nobody can find a lost heroine in the scrub but the aboriginal 'tracker,' and he will not lend himself to the scheme if it will interfere with the novelist's plot. The scrub stretches miles and miles in all directions, and looks like a level roof of bush-tops without a break or a crack in it—as seamless as a blanket, to all appearance. One might as well walk under water and hope to guess out a route and stick to it, I should think. Yet it is claimed that the aboriginal 'tracker' was able to hunt out people lost in the scrub. Also in the 'bush'; also in the desert; and even follow them over patches of bare rocks and over alluvial ground which had to all appearance been washed clear of footprints.

From reading Australian books and talking with the people, I became convinced that the aboriginal tracker's performances evince a craft, a penetration, a luminous sagacity, and a minuteness and accuracy of observation in the matter of detective-work not found in nearly so remarkable a degree in any other people, white or colored. In an official account of the blacks of Australia published by the government of Victoria, one reads that the aboriginal not only notices the faint marks left on the bark of a tree by the claws of a climbing opossum, but knows in some way or other whether the marks were made to-day or yesterday.

And there is the case, on record, where A., a settler, makes a bet with B., that B. may lose a cow as effectually as he can, and A. will produce an aboriginal who will find her. B. selects a cow and lets the tracker see the cow's footprint, then be put under guard. B. then drives the cow a few miles over a course which drifts in all directions, and frequently doubles back upon itself; and he selects difficult ground all the time, and once or twice even drives the cow through herds of other cows, and mingles her tracks in the wide confusion of theirs. He finally brings his cow home; the aboriginal is set at liberty, and at once moves around in a great circle, examining all cow-tracks until he finds the one he is after; then sets off and follows it throughout its erratic course, and ultimately tracks it to the stable where B. has hidden the cow. Now wherein does one cow-track differ from another? There must be a difference, or the tracker could not have performed the feat; a difference minute, shadowy, and not detectible by you or me, or by the late Sherlock Holmes, and yet discernible by a member of a race charged by some people with occupying the bottom place in the gradations of human intelligence.

10

Everything Comes to Him Who Waits

> It is easier to stay out than get out.
>
> —*Pudd'nhead Wilson's New Calendar*

The train was now exploring a beautiful hill country, and went twisting in and out through lovely little green valleys. There were several varieties of gum trees; among them many giants. Some of them were bodied and barked like the sycamore; some were of fantastic aspect, and reminded one of the quaint apple trees in Japanese pictures. And there was one peculiarly beautiful tree whose name and breed I did not know. The foliage seemed to consist of big bunches of pine-spines, the lower half of each bunch a rich brown or old-gold color, the upper half a most vivid and strenuous and shouting green. The effect was altogether bewitching. The tree was apparently rare. I should say that the first and last samples of it seen by us were not more than half an hour apart. There was another tree of striking aspect, a kind of pine, we were told. Its foliage was as fine as hair, apparently, and its mass sphered itself above the naked straight stem like an explosion of misty smoke. It was not a sociable sort; it did not gather in groups or couples, but each individual stood far away from its nearest neighbor. It scattered itself in this spacious and exclusive fashion about the slopes of swelling grassy great knolls, and stood in the full flood of the wonderful sunshine; and as far as you could see the tree itself you could also see the ink-black blot of its shadow on the shining green carpet at its feet.

On some part of this railway journey we saw gorse and broom—importations from England—and a gentleman who came into our compartment on a visit tried to tell me which was which; but as he didn't know, he had difficulty. He said he was ashamed of his ignorance, but that he had never been confronted with the question before during the fifty years and more that he had spent in Australia, and so he had never happened to get interested in the matter. But there was no need to be ashamed. The most of us have his defect. We take a natural interest in novelties, but it is against nature to take an interest in familiar things. The gorse and the broom were a fine accent in the landscape. Here and there they burst out in sudden conflagrations of vivid yellow against a background of sober or sombre color, with a so startling effect as to make a body catch his breath with the happy surprise of it. And then there was the wattle, a native bush or tree, an inspiring cloud of sumptuous yellow bloom. It is a favorite with the Australians, and has a fine fragrance, a quality usually wanting in Australian blossoms.

The gentleman who enriched me with the poverty of his information about the gorse and the broom told me that he came out from England a youth of twenty and entered the Province of South Australia with thirty-six shillings in his pocket—an adventurer without trade, profession, or friends, but with a clearly-defined purpose in his head: he would stay until he was worth £200, then go back home. He would allow himself five years for the accumulation of this fortune.

'That was more than fifty years ago,' said he. 'And here I am, yet.'

As he went out at the door he met a friend, and turned and introduced him to me, and the friend and I had a talk and a smoke. I spoke of the previous conversation and said there was something very pathetic about this half century of exile, and that I wished the £200 scheme had succeeded.

> 'With *him*? Oh, it did. It's not so sad a case. He is modest, and he left out some of the particulars. The lad reached South Australia just in time to help discover the Burra-Burra copper mines. They turned out £700,000 in the first three years. Up to now they have yielded £20,000,000. He has had his share. Before that boy had been in the country two years he could have gone home and bought a village; he could go now and buy a city, I think. No, there is nothing very pathetic about his case. He and his copper arrived at just a handy

time to save South Australia. It had got mashed pretty flat under the collapse of a land boom a while before.'

There it is again; picturesque history—Australia's specialty. In 1829 South Australia hadn't a white man in it. In 1836 the British Parliament erected it—still a solitude—into a Province, and gave it a governor and other governmental machinery. Speculators took hold, now, and inaugurated a vast land scheme, and invited immigration, encouraging it with lurid promises of sudden wealth. It was well worked in London; and bishops, statesmen, and all sorts of people made a rush for the land company's shares. Immigrants soon began to pour into the region of Adelaide and select town lots and farms in the sand and the mangrove swamps by the sea. The crowds continued to come, prices of land rose high, then higher and still higher, everybody was prosperous and happy, the boom swelled into gigantic proportions. A village of sheet iron huts and clapboard sheds sprang up in the sand, and in these wigwams fashion made display; richly-dressed ladies played on costly pianos, London swells in evening dress and patent-leather boots were abundant, and this fine society drank champagne, and in other ways conducted itself in this capital of humble sheds as it had been accustomed to do in the aristocratic quarters of the metropolis of the world. The provincial government put up expensive buildings for its own use, and a palace with gardens for the use of its governor. The governor had a guard, and maintained a court. Roads, wharves, and hospitals were built. All this on credit, on paper, on wind, on inflated and fictitious values—on the boom's moonshine, in fact.

This went on handsomely during four or five years. Then of a sudden came a smash. Bills for a huge amount drawn by the governor upon the Treasury were dishonored, the land company's credit went up in smoke, a panic followed, values fell with a rush, the frightened immigrants seized their grips and fled to other lands, leaving behind them a good imitation of a solitude, where lately had been a buzzing and populous hive of men.

Adelaide was indeed almost empty; its population had fallen to 3,000. During two years or more the death-trance continued. Prospect of revival there was none; hope of it ceased. Then, as suddenly as the paralysis had come, came the resurrection from it. Those astonishingly rich copper mines were discovered, and the corpse got up and danced.

The wool production began to grow; grain-raising followed—followed so vigorously, too, that four or five years after the copper discovery, this little colony, which had had to import its breadstuffs formerly, and pay hard prices for them—once $50 a barrel for flour—had become an exporter of grain. The prosperities continued. After many years Providence, desiring to show especial regard for New South Wales and exhibit a loving interest in its welfare which should certify to all nations the recognition of that colony's conspicuous righteousness and distinguished well-deserving, conferred upon it that treasury of inconceivable riches, Broken Hill; and South Australia went over the border and took it, giving thanks.

Among our passengers was an American with a unique vocation. Unique is a strong word, but I use it justifiably if I did not misconceive what the American told me; for I understood him to say that in the world there was not another man engaged in the business which he was following. He was buying the kangaroo-skin crop; buying all of it, both the Australian crop and the Tasmanian; and buying it for an American house in New York. The prices were not high, as there was no competition, but the year's aggregate of skins would cost him £30,000. I had had the idea that the kangaroo was about extinct in Tasmania and well thinned out on the continent. In America the skins are tanned and made into shoes. After the tanning, the leather takes a new name—which I have forgotten—I only remember that the new name does not indicate that the kangaroo furnishes the leather. There was a German competition for a while, some years ago, but that has ceased. The Germans failed to arrive at the secret of tanning the skins successfully, and they withdrew from the business. Now then, I suppose that I have seen a man whose occupation is really entitled to bear that high epithet—unique. And I suppose that there is not another occupation in the world that is restricted to the hands of a sole person. I can think of no instance of it. There is more than one Pope, there is more than one Emperor, there is even more than one living god, walking upon the earth and worshiped in all sincerity by large populations of men. I have seen and talked with two of these Beings myself in India, and I have the autograph of one of them. It can come good, by and by, I reckon, if I attach it to a 'permit.'

Approaching Adelaide we dismounted from the train, as the French say, and were driven in an open carriage over the hills and along their slopes to the city. It was an excursion of an hour or two, and the charm of it could not be overstated, I think. The road wound around gaps and gorges, and offered all varieties of scenery and prospect—mountains, crags, country homes, gardens, forests—color, color, color everywhere, and the air fine and fresh, the skies blue, and not a shred of cloud to mar the downpour of the brilliant sunshine. And finally the mountain gateway opened, and the immense plain lay spread out below and stretching away into dim distances on every hand, soft and delicate and dainty and beautiful. On its near edge reposed the city.

We descended and entered. There was nothing to remind one of the humble capital, of huts and sheds of the long-vanished day of the land-boom. No, this was a modern city, with wide streets, compactly built; with fine homes everywhere, embowered in foliage and flowers, and with imposing masses of public buildings nobly grouped and architecturally beautiful.

There was prosperity, in the air; for another boom was on. Providence, desiring to show especial regard for the neighboring colony on the west—called Western Australia—and exhibit a loving interest in its welfare which should certify to all nations the recognition of that colony's conspicuous righteousness and distinguished well-deserving, had recently conferred upon it that majestic treasury of golden riches, Coolgardie; and now South Australia had gone around the corner and taken it, giving thanks. Everything comes to him who is patient and good, and waits.

But South Australia deserves much, for apparently she is a hospitable home for every alien who chooses to come; and for his religion, too. She has a population, as per the latest census, of only 320,000-odd, and yet her varieties of religion indicate the presence within her borders of samples of people from pretty nearly every part of the globe you can think of. Tabulated, these varieties of religion make a remarkable show. One would have to go far to find its match. I copy here this cosmopolitan curiosity, and it comes from the published census:

Church of England,	89,271
Roman Catholic,	47,179
Wesleyan,	49,159
Lutheran,	23,328
Presbyterian,	18,206
Congregationalist,	11,882
Bible Christian,	15,762
Primitive Methodist,	11,654
Baptist,	17,547
Christian Brethren,	465
Methodist New Connexion,	39
Unitarian,	688
Church of Christ,	3,367
Society of Friends,	100
Salvation Army,	4,356
New Jerusalem Church,	168
Jews,	840
Protestants (undefined),	6,532

Mohammedans,	299
Confucians, etc.,	3,884
Other religions,	1,719
Object,	6,940
Not stated,	8,046
Total,	320,431

The item in the above list 'Other religions' includes the following as returned:

Agnostics,	50
Atheists,	22
Believers in Christ,	4
Buddhists,	52
Calvinists,	46
Christadelphians,	134
Christians,	308
Christ's Chapel,	9
Christian Israelites,	2
Christian Socialists,	6
Church of God,	6
Cosmopolitans,	3
Deists,	14
Evangelists,	60
Exclusive Brethren,	8
Free Church,	21
Free Methodists,	5
Freethinkers,	258
Followers of Christ,	8
Gospel Meetings,	8
Greek Church,	44
Infidels,	9
Maronites,	2
Memnonists,	1

Moravians,	139
Mormons,	4
Naturalists,	2
Orthodox,	4
Others (indefinite),	17
Pagans,	20
Pantheists,	3
Plymouth Brethren,	111
Rationalists,	4
Reformers,	7
Secularists,	12
Seventh-day Adventists,	203
Shaker,	1
Shintoists,	24
Spiritualists,	37
Theosophists,	9
Town (City) Mission,	16
Welsh Church,	27
Huguenot,	2
Hussite,	1
Zoroastrians,	2
Zwinglian,	1

About 64 roads to the other world. You see how healthy the religious atmosphere is. Anything can live in it. Agnostics, Atheists, Freethinkers, Infidels, Mormons, Pagans, Indefinites: they are all there. And all the big sects of the world can do more than merely live in it: they can spread, flourish, prosper. All except the Spiritualists and the Theosophists. That is the most curious feature of this curious table. What is the matter with the specter? Why do they puff him away? He is a welcome toy everywhere else in the world.

11

The Laughing Jackass

Pity is for the living, Envy is for the dead.

—*Pudd'nhead Wilson's New Calendar*

The successor of the sheet-iron hamlet of the mangrove marshes has that other Australian specialty, the Botanical Gardens. We cannot have these paradises. The best we could do would be to cover a vast acreage under glass and apply steam heat. But it would be inadequate, the lacks would still be so great: the confined sense, the sense of suffocation, the atmospheric dimness, the sweaty heat—these would all be there, in place of the Australian openness to the sky, the sunshine and the breeze. Whatever will grow under glass with us will flourish rampantly out of doors in Australia.[1] When the white man came the continent was nearly as poor, in variety of vegetation, as the desert of Sahara; now it has everything that grows on the earth.

In fact, not Australia only, but all Australasia has levied tribute upon the flora of the rest of the world; and wherever one goes the results appear, in gardens private and public, in the woodsy walls of the highways, and in even the forests. If you see a curious or beautiful tree or bush or flower, and ask about it, the people, answering, usually name a foreign country as the place of its origin—India, Africa, Japan, China, England, America, Java, Sumatra, New Guinea, Polynesia, and so on.

In the Zoological Gardens of Adelaide I saw the only laughing jackass that ever showed any disposition to be courteous to me. This one opened his head wide and laughed like a demon; or like a maniac who was consumed with humorous scorn over a cheap and degraded pun. It was a very human laugh. If he had been out of sight I could have believed that the laughter came from a man. It is an odd-looking bird, with a head and beak that are much too large for its body. In time man will exterminate the rest of the wild creatures of Australia, but this one will probably survive, for man is his friend and lets him alone. Man always has a good reason for his charities towards wild things, human or animal—when he has any. In this case the bird is spared because he kills snakes. If L. J. will take my advice he will not kill all of them.

In that garden I also saw the wild Australian dog—the dingo. He was a beautiful creature—shapely, graceful, a little wolfish in some of his aspects, but with a most friendly eye and sociable disposition. The dingo is not an importation; he was present in great force when the whites first came to the continent. It may be that he is the oldest dog in the universe; his origin, his descent, the place where his ancestors first appeared, are as unknown and as untraceable as are the camel's. He is the most precious dog in the world, for he does not bark. But in an evil hour he got to raiding the sheep-runs to appease his hunger, and that sealed his doom. He is hunted, now, just as if he were a wolf. He has been sentenced to extermination, and the sentence will be carried out. This is all right, and not objectionable. The world was made for man—the white man.

South Australia is confusingly named. All of the colonies have a southern exposure except one—Queensland. Properly speaking, South Australia is *middle* Australia. It extends straight up through the center of the continent like the middle board in a center-table. It is 2,000 miles high, from south to north, and about a third as wide. A wee little spot down in its southeastern corner contains eight or nine-tenths of its population; the other one or two-tenths are elsewhere—as elsewhere as they could be in the United States with all the country between Denver and Chicago, and Canada and the Gulf of Mexico to scatter over. There is plenty of room.

A telegraph line stretches straight up north through that 2,000 miles of wilderness and desert from Adelaide to Port Darwin on the edge of the upper ocean. South Australia built the line; and did it in 1871–2 when her population numbered only 185,000. It was a great work; for there were no roads, no paths; 1,300 miles of the route had been traversed but once before by white men; provisions, wire, and poles had to be carried over immense stretches of desert; wells had to be dug along the route to supply the men and cattle with water.

A cable had been previously laid from Port Darwin to Java and thence to India, and there was telegraphic communication with England from India. And so, if Adelaide could make connection with Port Darwin it meant connection with the whole world. The enterprise succeeded. One could watch the London markets daily, now; the profit to the wool-growers of Australia was instant and enormous.

A telegram from Melbourne to San Francisco covers approximately 20,000 miles—the equivalent of five-sixths of the way around the globe. It has to halt along the way a good many times and be repeated; still, but little time is lost. These halts, and the distances between them, are here tabulated.[2]

	Miles
Melbourne–Mount Gambier	300
Mount Gambier–Adelaide	270
Adelaide–Port Augusta	200
Port Augusta–Alice Springs	1,036
Alice Springs–Port Darwin	898
Port Darwin–Banjoewangie	1,150
Banjoewangie–Batavia	480
Batavia–Singapore	553
Singapore–Penang	399
Penang–Madras	1,280
Madras–Bombay	650
Bombay–Aden	1,662
Aden–Suez	1,346
Suez–Alexandria	224

Alexandria–Malta	828
Malta–Gibraltar	1,008
Gibraltar–Falmouth	1,061
Falmouth–London	350
London–New York	2,500
New York–San Francisco	3,500

I was in Adelaide again, some months later, and saw the multitudes gather in the neighboring city of Glenelg to commemorate the Reading of the Proclamation—in 1836—which founded the Province. If I have at any time called it a Colony, I withdraw the discourtesy. It is not a Colony, it is a Province; and officially so. Moreover, it is the only one so named in Australasia. There was great enthusiasm; it was the Province's national holiday, its Fourth of July, so to speak. It is the pre-eminent holiday; and that is saying much, in a country where they seem to have a most un-English mania for holidays. Mainly they are workingmen's holidays; for in South Australia the working-man is sovereign; his vote is the desire of the politician—indeed, it is the very breath of the politician's being; the parliament exists to deliver the will of the workingman, and the government exists to execute it. The workingman is a great power everywhere in Australia, but South Australia is his paradise. He has had a hard time in this world, and has earned a paradise. I am glad he has found it. The holidays there are frequent enough to be bewildering to the stranger. I tried to get the hang of the system, but was not able to do it.

You have seen that the Province is tolerant, religious-wise. It is so politically, also. One of the speakers at the Commemoration banquet—the Minister of Public Works—was an American, born and reared in New England. There is nothing narrow about the Province, politically, or in any other way that I know of. Sixty-four religions and a Yankee cabinet minister. No amount of horse-racing can damn this community.

The mean temperature of the Province is 62°. The death-rate is 13 in the 1,000—about half what it is in the city of New York, I should think, and New York is a healthy city. Thirteen is the death-rate for the average citizen of the Province, but there seems to be no death-rate for the old people. There were people at the Commemoration banquet who could remember Cromwell. There were six of them. These Old Settlers had all been present at the original Reading of the Proclamation, in 1836. They showed signs of the blightings and blastings of time, in their outward aspect, but they were young within; young and cheerful, and ready to talk; ready to talk, and talk all you wanted; in their turn, and out of it. They were down for six speeches, and they made 42. The governor and the cabinet and the mayor were down for 42 speeches, and they made 6. They have splendid grit, the Old Settlers, splendid staying power. But they do not hear well, and when they see the mayor going through motions which they recognize as the introducing of a speaker, they think they are the one, and they all get up together, and begin to respond, in the most animated way; and the more the mayor gesticulates, and shouts 'Sit down! Sit down!' the more they take it for applause, and the more excited and reminiscent and enthusiastic they get; and next, when they see the whole house laughing and crying, three of them think it is about the bitter old-time hardships they are describing, and the other three think the laughter is caused by the jokes they have been uncorking—jokes of the vintage of 1836—and then the way they *do* go on! And finally when ushers come and plead, and beg, and gently and reverently crowd them down into their seats, they say, 'Oh, I'm not tired—I could bang along a week!' and they sit there looking simple and childlike, and gentle, and proud of their oratory, and wholly unconscious of what is going on at the other end of the room. And so one of the great dignitaries gets a chance, and begins his carefully prepared speech, impressively and with solemnity—

> When we, now great and prosperous and powerful, bow our heads in reverent wonder in the contemplation of those sublimities of energy, of wisdom, of forethought, of—

Up come the immortal six again, in a body, with a joyous 'Hey, I've thought of another one!' and at it they go, with might and main, hearing not a whisper of the pandemonium that salutes them, but taking all the visible violences for applause, as before, and hammering joyously away till the imploring ushers pray them into their seats again. And a pity, too; for those lovely old boys did so enjoy living their heroic youth over, in these days of their honored antiquity; and certainly the things they had to tell were usually worth the telling and the hearing.

It was a stirring spectacle; stirring in more ways than one, for it was amazingly funny, and at the same time deeply pathetic; for they had seen so much, these time-worn veterans, and had suffered so much; and had built so strongly and well, and laid the foundations of their commonwealth so deep, in liberty and tolerance; and had lived to see the structure rise to such state and dignity and hear themselves so praised for honorable work.

One of these old gentlemen told me some things of interest afterward; things about the aboriginals, mainly. He thought them intelligent—remarkably so in some directions—and he said that along with their unpleasant qualities they had some exceedingly good ones; and he considered it a great pity that the race had died out. He instanced their invention of the boomerang and the 'weet-weet' as evidences of their brightness; and as another evidence of it he said he had never seen a white man who had cleverness enough to learn to do the miracles with those two toys that the aboriginals achieved. He said that even the smartest whites had been obliged to confess that they could not learn the trick of the boomerang in perfection; that it had possibilities which they could not master. The white man could not control its motions, could not make it obey him; but the aboriginal could. He told me some wonderful things—some almost incredible things—which he had seen the blacks do with the boomerang and the weet-weet. They have been confirmed to me since by other early settlers and by trustworthy books.

It is contended—and may be said to be conceded—that the boomerang was known to certain savage tribes in Europe in Roman times. In support of this, Virgil and two other Roman poets are quoted. It is also contended that it was known to the ancient Egyptians.

One of two things is then apparent: either some one with a boomerang arrived in Australia in the days of antiquity before European knowledge of the thing had been lost, or the Australian aboriginal reinvented it. It will take some time to find out which of these two propositions is the fact. But there is no hurry.

12

An Accurate Judgment of an Idiot

> It is by the goodness of God that
> in our country we have those three
> unspeakably precious things: freedom of
> speech, freedom of conscience, and the
> prudence never to practice either of them.
>
> —*Pudd'nhead Wilson's New Calendar*

From diary:

Mr. G. called. I had not seen him since Nauheim, Germany—several years ago; the time that the cholera broke out at Hamburg. We talked of the people we had known there, or had casually met; and G. said:

> 'Do you remember my introducing you to an earl—the Earl of C.?'
>
> 'Yes. That was the last time I saw you. You and he were in a carriage, just starting—belated—for the train. I remember it.'

'I remember it too, because of a thing which happened then which I was not looking for. He had told me a while before, about a remarkable and interesting Californian whom he had met and who was a friend of yours, and said that if he should ever meet you he would ask you for some particulars about that Californian. The subject was not mentioned that day at Nauheim, for we were hurrying away, and there was no time; but the thing that surprised me was this: when I introduced you, you said, "I am glad to meet your lordship—again." The "again" was the surprise. He is a little hard of hearing, and didn't catch that word, and I thought you hadn't intended that he should. As we drove off I had only time to say, "Why, what do you know about him?" and I understood you to say, "Oh, nothing, except that he is the quickest judge of—" Then we were gone, and I didn't get the rest. I wondered what it was that he was such a quick judge of. I have thought of it many times since, and still wondered what it could be. He and I talked it over, but could not guess it out. He thought it must be fox-hounds or horses, for he is a good judge of those—no one is a better. But *you* couldn't know that, because you didn't know *him*; you had mistaken him for some one else; it must be that, he said, because he knew you had never met him before. And of course you hadn't—had you?'

'Yes, I had.'

'Is that so? Where?'

'At a fox-hunt, in England.'

'How curious that is. Why, he hadn't the least recollection of it. Had you any conversation with him?'

'Some—yes.'

'Well, it left not the least impression upon him. What did you talk about?'

'About the fox. I think that was all.'

'Why, *that* would interest him; that ought to have left an impression. What did *he* talk about?'

'The fox.'

'It's very curious. I don't understand it. Did what he said leave an impression upon you?'

'Yes. It showed me that he was a quick judge of—however, I will tell you all about it, then you will understand. It was a quarter of a century ago—1873 or '74. I had an American friend in London named F., who was fond of hunting, and his friends the Blanks invited him and me to come out to a hunt and be their guests at their country place. In the morning the mounts were provided, but when I saw the horses I changed my mind and asked permission to walk. I had never seen an English hunter before, and it seemed to me that I could hunt a fox safer on the ground. I had always been diffident about horses, anyway, even those of the common altitudes, and I did not feel competent to hunt on a horse that went on stilts. So then Mrs. Blank came to my help and said I could go with her in the dog-cart and we would drive to a place she knew of, and there we should have a good glimpse of the hunt as it went by.

'When we got to that place I got out and went and leaned my elbows on a low stone wall which enclosed a turfy and beautiful great field with heavy wood on all its sides except ours. Mrs. Blank sat in the dog-cart fifty yards away, which was as near as she could get with the vehicle. I was full of interest, for I had never seen a fox-hunt. I waited, dreaming and imagining, in the deep stillness and impressive tranquility which reigned in that retired spot. Presently, from away off in the forest on the left, a mellow bugle-note came floating; then all of a sudden a multitude of dogs burst out of that forest and went tearing by and disappeared in the forest on the right; there was a pause, and then a cloud of horsemen in black caps and crimson coats plunged out of the left-hand forest and went flaming across the field like a prairie-fire, a stirring sight to see. There was one man ahead of the rest, and he came spurring straight at me. He was fiercely excited. It was fine to see him ride; he was a master horseman. He came like a storm till he was within seven feet of me, where I was leaning on the wall, then he stood his horse straight up in the air on his hind toe-nails, and shouted like a demon:

'"Which way'd the fox go?"

'I didn't much like the tone, but I did not let on; for he was excited, you know. But I was calm; so I said softly, and without acrimony:

'"*Which* fox?"

'It seemed to anger him. I don't know why; and he thundered out:

"'*Which* fox? Why, *the* fox? Which way did the *fox* go?"

'I said, with great gentleness—even argumentatively:

"'If you could be a little more definite—a little less vague—because I am a stranger, and there are many foxes, as you will know even better than I, and unless I know which one it is that you desire to identify, and—"

"'You're certainly the damdest idiot that has escaped in a thousand years!" and he snatched his great horse around as easily as I would snatch a cat, and was away like a hurricane. A very excitable man.

'I went back to Mrs. Blank, and *she* was excited, too—oh, all alive. She said:

"'He *spoke* to you!—*didn't* he?"

"'Yes, it is what happened."

"'I *knew* it! I couldn't hear what he said, but I *knew* be spoke to you! Do you know who it was? It was Lord C., and he is Master of the Buckhounds! Tell me—what do you think of him?"

"'Him? Well, for sizing-up a stranger, he's got the most sudden and accurate judgment of any man I ever saw."

'It pleased her. I thought it would.'

G. got away from Nauheim just in time to escape being shut in by the quarantine-bars on the frontiers; and so did we, for we left the next day. But G. had a great deal of trouble in getting by the Italian custom-house, and we should have fared likewise but for the thoughtfulness of our consul-general in Frankfort. He introduced me to the Italian consul-general, and I brought away from that consulate a letter which made our way smooth. It was a dozen lines merely commending me in a general way to the courtesies of servants in his Italian Majesty's service, but it was more powerful than it looked. In addition to a raft of ordinary baggage, we had six or eight trunks which were filled exclusively with dutiable stuff—household goods purchased in Frankfort for use in Florence, where we had taken a house. I was going to ship these through by express; but at the last moment an order went throughout Germany forbidding the moving of any parcels by train unless the owner went with them. This was a bad outlook. We must take these things along, and the delay sure to be caused by the examination of them in the custom-house might lose us our train. I imagined all sorts of terrors, and enlarged them steadily as we approached the Italian frontier. We were six in number, clogged with all that baggage, and I was courier for the party—the most incapable one they ever employed.

We arrived, and pressed with the crowd into the immense custom-house, and the usual worries began; everybody crowding to the counter and begging to have his baggage examined first, and all hands clattering and chattering at once. It seemed to me that I could do nothing; it would be better to give it all up and go away and leave the baggage. I couldn't speak the language; I should never accomplish anything.

Just then a tall handsome man in a fine uniform was passing by and I knew he must be the station-master—and that reminded me of my letter. I ran to him and put it into his hands. He took it out of the envelope, and the moment his eye caught the royal coat of arms printed at its top, he took off his cap and made a beautiful bow to me, and said in English—

'Which is your baggage? Please show it to me.'

I showed him the mountain. Nobody was disturbing it; nobody was interested in it; all the family's attempts to get attention to it had failed—except in the case of one of the trunks containing the dutiable goods. It was just being opened. My officer said—

'There, let that alone! Lock it. Now chalk it. Chalk all of the lot. Now please come and show me the hand-baggage.'

He plowed through the waiting crowd, I following, to the counter, and he gave orders again, in his emphatic military way—

'Chalk these. Chalk *all* of them.'

Then he took off his cap and made that beautiful bow again, and went his way. By this time these attentions had attracted the wonder of that acre of passengers, and the whisper had gone around that the royal family were present getting their baggage chalked; and as we passed down in review on our way to the door, I was conscious of a pervading atmosphere of envy which gave me deep satisfaction.

But soon there was an accident. My overcoat pockets were stuffed with German cigars and linen packages of American smoking tobacco, and a porter was following us around with this overcoat on his arm, and gradually getting it upside down. Just as I, in the rear of my family, moved by the sentinels at the door, about three hatfuls of the tobacco tumbled out on the floor. One of the soldiers pounced upon it, gathered it up in his arms, pointed back whence I had come, and marched me ahead of him past that long wall of passengers again—he chattering and exulting like a devil, they smiling in peaceful joy, and I trying to look as if my pride was not hurt, and as if I did not mind being brought to shame before these pleased people who had so lately envied me. But at heart I was cruelly humbled.

When I had been marched two-thirds of the long distance and the misery of it was at the worst, the stately station-master stepped out from somewhere, and the soldier left me and darted after him and overtook him; and I could see by the soldier's excited gestures that he was betraying to him the whole shabby business. The station-master was plainly very angry. He came striding down toward me, and when he was come near he began to pour out a stream of indignant Italian; then suddenly took off his hat and made that beautiful bow and said—

> 'Oh, it is *you*! I beg a thousands pardons! This idiot here—'

He turned to the exulting soldier and burst out with a flood of white-hot Italian lava, and the next moment he was bowing, and the soldier and I were moving in procession again—he in the lead and ashamed, this time, I with my chin up. And so we marched by the crowd of fascinated passengers, and I went forth to the train with the honors of war. Tobacco and all.

13

Pudding with Arsenic Revenge

> Man will do many things to get himself
> loved, he will do all things to get
> himself envied.
>
> —*Pudd'nhead Wilson's New Calendar*

Before I saw Australia I had never heard of the 'weet-weet' at all. I met but few men who had seen it thrown—at least I met but few who mentioned having seen it thrown. Roughly described, it is a fat wooden cigar with its butt-end fastened to a flexible twig. The whole thing is only a couple of feet long, and weighs less than two ounces. This feather—so to call it—is not thrown through the air, but is flung with an underhanded throw and made to strike the ground a little way in front of the thrower; then it glances and makes a long skip; glances again, skips again, and again and again, like the flat stone which a boy sends skating over the water. The water is smooth, and the stone has a good chance; so a strong man may make it travel fifty or seventy-five yards; but the weet-weet has no such good chance, for it strikes sand, grass, and earth in its course. Yet an expert aboriginal has sent it a measured distance of *two hundred and twenty yards*. It would have gone even further but it encountered rank ferns and underwood on its passage and they damaged its speed. Two hundred and twenty yards; and so weightless a toy—a mouse on the end of a bit of wire, in effect; and not sailing through the accommodating air, but encountering grass and sand and stuff at every jump. It looks wholly impossible; but Mr. Brough Smyth saw the feat and did the measuring, and set down the facts in his book about aboriginal life, which he wrote by command of the Victorian Government.

What is the secret of the feat? No one explains. It cannot be physical strength, for that could not drive such a feather-weight any distance. It must be art. But no one explains what the art of it is; nor how it gets around that law of nature which says you shall not throw any two-ounce thing 220 yards, either through the air or bumping along the ground. Rev. J. G. Woods says:

> The distance to which the weet-weet or kangaroo-rat can be thrown is truly astonishing. I have seen an Australian stand at one side of Kennington Oval and throw the kangaroo rat completely across it. (Width of Kensington Oval not stated.) It darts through the air with the sharp and menacing hiss of a rifle-ball, its greatest height from the ground

being some seven or eight feet . . . When properly thrown it looks just like a living animal leaping along . . . Its movements have a wonderful resemblance to the long leaps of a kangaroo-rat fleeing in alarm, with its long tail trailing behind it.

The Old Settler said that he had seen distances made by the weet-weet, in the early days, which almost convinced him that it was as extraordinary an instrument as the boomerang.

There must have been a large distribution of acuteness among those naked skinny aboriginals, or they couldn't have been such unapproachable trackers and boomerangers and weet-weeters. It must have been race-aversion that put upon them a good deal of the low-rate intellectual reputation which they bear and have borne this long time in the world's estimate of them.

They were lazy—always lazy. Perhaps that was their trouble. It is a killing defect. Surely they could have invented and built a competent house, but they didn't. And they could have invented and developed the agricultural arts, but they didn't. They went naked and houseless, and lived on fish and grubs and worms and wild fruits, and were just plain savages, for all their smartness.

With a country as big as the United States to live and multiply in, and with no epidemic diseases among them till the white man came with those and his other appliances of civilization, it is quite probable that there was never a day in his history when he could muster 100,000 of his race in all Australia. He diligently and deliberately kept population down by infanticide—largely; but mainly by certain other methods. He did not need to practise these artificialities any more after the white man came. The white man knew ways of keeping down population which were worth several of his. The white man knew ways of reducing a native population 80 per cent in 20 years. The native had never seen anything as fine as that before.

For example, there is the case of the country now called Victoria—a country eighty times as large as Rhode Island, as I have already said. By the best official guess there were 4,500 aboriginals in it when the whites came along in the middle of the 'Thirties. Of these, 1,000 lived in Gippsland, a patch of territory the size of fifteen or sixteen Rhode Islands: they did not diminish as fast as some of the other communities; indeed, at the end of forty years there were still 200 of them left. The Geelong tribe diminished more satisfactorily: from 173 persons it faded to 34 in twenty years; at the end of another twenty the tribe numbered one person altogether. The two Melbourne tribes could muster almost 300 when the white man came; they could muster but twenty, thirty-seven years later, in 1875. In that year there were still odds and ends of tribes scattered about the colony of Victoria, but I was told that natives of full blood are very scarce now. It is said that the aboriginals continue in some force in the huge territory called Queensland.

The early whites were not used to savages. They could not understand the primary law of savage life: that if a man do you a wrong, his whole tribe is responsible—each individual of it—and you may take your change out of any individual of it, without bothering to seek out the guilty one. When a white killed an aboriginal, the tribe applied the ancient law, and killed the first white they came across. To the whites this was a monstrous thing. Extermination seemed to be the proper medicine for such creatures as this. They did not kill all the blacks, but they promptly killed enough of them to make their own persons safe. From the dawn of civilization down to this day the white man has always used that very precaution. Mrs. Campbell Praed lived in Queensland, as a child, in the early days, and in her *Sketches of Australian Life*, we get informing pictures of the early struggles of the white and the black to reform each other.

Speaking of pioneer days in the mighty wilderness of Queensland, Mrs. Praed says:

> At first the natives retreated before the whites; and, except that they every now and then speared a beast in one of the herds, gave little cause for uneasiness. But, as the number of squatters increased, each one taking up miles of country and bringing two or three men in his train, so that shepherds' huts and stockmen's camps lay far apart, and defenseless in the midst of hostile tribes, the Blacks' depredations became more frequent and murder was no unusual event.
>
> The loneliness of the Australian bush can hardly be painted in words. Here extends mile after mile of primeval forest where perhaps foot of white man has never trod—interminable vistas where the eucalyptus trees rear their lofty trunks and spread

forth their lanky limbs, from which the red gum oozes and hangs in fantastic pendants like crimson stalactites; ravines along the sides of which the long-bladed grass grows rankly; level untimbered plains alternating with undulating tracts of pasture, here and there broken by a stony ridge, steep gully, or dried-up creek. All wild, vast and desolate; all the same monotonous gray coloring, except where the wattle, when in blossom, shows patches of feathery gold, or a belt of scrub lies green, glossy, and impenetrable as Indian jungle.

The solitude seems intensified by the strange sounds of reptiles, birds, and insects, and by the absence of larger creatures; of which in the daytime, the only audible signs are the stampede of a herd of kangaroo, or the rustle of a wallabi, or a dingo stirring the grass as it creeps to its lair. But there are the whirring of locusts, the demoniac chuckle of the laughing jack-ass, the screeching of cockatoos and parrots, the hissing of the frilled lizard, and the buzzing of innumerable insects hidden under the dense undergrowth. And then at night, the melancholy wailing of the curlews, the dismal howling of dingoes, the discordant croaking of tree-frogs, might well shake the nerves of the solitary watcher.

That is the theater for the drama. When you comprehend one or two other details, you will perceive how well suited for trouble it was, and how loudly it invited it. The cattlemen's stations were scattered over that profound wilderness miles and miles apart—at each station half a dozen persons. There was a plenty of cattle, the black natives were always ill-nourished and hungry. The land belonged to *them.* The whites had not bought it, and couldn't buy it; for the tribes had no chiefs, nobody in authority, nobody competent to sell and convey; and the tribes themselves had no comprehension of the idea of transferable ownership of land. The ousted owners were despised by the white interlopers, and this opinion was not hidden under a bushel. More promising materials for a tragedy could not have been collated. Let Mrs. Praed speak:

> At Nie Nie station, one dark night, the unsuspecting hut-keeper, having, as he believed, secured himself against assault, was lying wrapped in his blankets sleeping profoundly. The Blacks crept stealthily down the chimney and battered in his skull while he slept.

One could guess the whole drama from that little text. The curtain was up. It would not fall until the mastership of one party or the other was determined—and permanently:

> There was treachery on both sides. The Blacks killed the Whites when they found them defenseless, and the Whites slew the Blacks in a wholesale and promiscuous fashion which offended against my childish sense of justice.
>   . . . They were regarded as little above the level of brutes, and in some cases *were destroyed like vermin.*

Here is an instance. A squatter, whose station was surrounded by Blacks, whom he suspected to be hostile and from whom he feared an attack, parleyed with them from his house-door. He told them it was Christmas-time—a time at which all men, black or white, feasted; that there were flour, sugar-plums, good things in plenty in the store, and that he would make for them such a pudding as they had never dreamed of—a great pudding of which all might eat and be filled. The Blacks listened and were lost. The pudding was made and distributed. Next morning there was howling in the camp, for it had been sweetened with sugar and arsenic!

The white man's spirit was right, but his method was wrong. His spirit was the spirit which the civilized white has always exhibited toward the savage, but the use of poison was a departure from custom. True, it was merely a technical departure, not a real one; still, it was a departure, and therefore a mistake, in my opinion. It was better, kinder, swifter, and much more humane than a number of the methods which have been sanctified by custom, but that does not justify its employment. That is, it does not wholly justify it. Its unusual nature makes it stand out and attract an amount of attention which it is not entitled to. It takes hold upon morbid imaginations and they work it up into a sort of exhibition of cruelty, and this smirches the good name of our civilization, whereas one of the old harsher methods would have had no such effect because usage has made those methods familiar to us and innocent. In many countries we have chained the savage and starved him to death; and this we do not care for, because custom has inured us to it; yet a quick death by poison is lovingkindness to it. In many countries we have burned the savage at the stake; and this we do not care for, because custom has inured us to it; yet a quick death is lovingkindness to it. In more than one country we have hunted the savage and his little children and their mother with dogs and guns through the woods and swamps for an afternoon's sport, and filled the region with happy laughter over their sprawling and stumbling flight, and their wild supplications for mercy; but this method we do not mind, because custom has inured us to it; yet a quick death by poison is lovingkindness to it. In many countries we have taken the savage's land from him, and made him our slave, and lashed him every day, and broken his pride, and made death his only friend, and overworked him till he dropped in his tracks; and this we do not care for, because custom has inured us to it; yet a quick death by poison is lovingkindness to it. In the Matabeleland to-day—why, there we are confining ourselves to sanctified custom, we Rhodes-Beit millionaires in South Africa and Dukes in London; and nobody cares, because we are used to the old holy customs, and all we ask is that no notice-inviting new ones shall be intruded upon the attention of our comfortable consciences. Mrs. Praed says of the poisoner, 'That squatter deserves to have his name handed down to the contempt of posterity.'

I am sorry to hear her say that. I myself blame him for one thing, and severely, but I stop there. I blame him for the indiscretion of introducing a novelty which was calculated to attract attention to our civilization. There was no occasion to do that. It was his duty, and it is every loyal man's duty to protect that heritage in every way he can; and the best way to do that is to attract attention elsewhere. The squatter's judgment was bad—that is plain; but his heart was right. He is almost the only pioneering representative of civilization in history who has risen above the prejudices of his caste and his heredity and tried to introduce the element of mercy into the superior race's dealings with the savage. His name is lost, and it is a pity; for it deserves to be handed down to posterity with homage and reverence.

This paragraph is from a London journal:

> To learn what France is doing to spread the blessings of civilization in her distant dependencies we may turn with advantage to New Caledonia. With a view to attracting free settlers to that penal colony, M. Feillet, the Governor, forcibly expropriated the Kanaka cultivators from the best of their plantations, with a derisory compensation, in spite of the protests of the Council General of the island. Such immigrants as could be induced to cross the seas thus found themselves in possession of thousands of coffee, cocoa, banana, and breadfruit trees, the raising of which had cost the wretched natives years of toil whilst the latter had a few five-franc pieces to spend in the liquor stores of Noumea.

You observe the combination? It is robbery, humiliation, and slow, slow murder, through poverty and the white man's whisky. The savage's gentle friend, the savage's noble friend, the only magnanimous and unselfish friend the savage has ever had, was not there with the merciful swift release of his poisoned pudding.

There are many humorous things in the world; among them the white man's notion that he is less savage than the other savages.

14

Dodging Balls

> Nothing is so ignorant as a man's left
> hand, except a lady's watch.
>
> —*Pudd'nhead Wilson's New Calendar*

You notice that Mrs. Praed knows her art. She can place a thing before you so that you can see it. She is not alone in that. Australia is fertile in writers whose books are faithful mirrors of the life of the country and of its history. The materials were surprisingly rich, both in quality and in mass, and Marcus Clarke, Ralph Boldrewood, Gordon, Kendall, and the others, have built out of them a brilliant and vigorous literature, and one which must endure. Materials—there is no end to them! Why, a literature might be made out of the aboriginal all by himself, his character and ways are so freckled with varieties—varieties not staled by familiarity, but new to us. You do not need to invent any picturesquenesses; whatever you want in that line he can furnish you; and they will not be fancies and doubtful, but realities and authentic. In his history, as preserved by the white man's official records, he is everything—everything that a human creature can be. He covers the entire ground. He is a coward—there are a thousand facts to prove it. He is brave—there are a thousand facts to prove it. He is treacherous—oh, beyond imagination! He is faithful, loyal, true—the white man's records supply you with a harvest of instances of it that are noble, worshipful, and pathetically beautiful. He kills the starving stranger who comes begging for food and shelter—there is proof of it. He succors, and feeds, and guides to safety, to-day, the lost stranger who fired on him only yesterday—there is proof of it. He takes his reluctant bride by force, he courts her with a club, then loves her faithfully through a long life—it is of record. He gathers to himself another wife by the same processes, beats and bangs her as a daily diversion, and by and by lays down his life in defending her from some outside harm—it is of record. He will face a hundred hostiles to rescue one of his children, and will kill another of his children because the family is large enough without it. His delicate stomach turns, at certain details of the white man's food; but he likes over-ripe fish, and brazed dog, and cat, and rat, and will eat his own uncle with relish. He is a sociable animal, yet he turns aside and hides behind his shield when his mother-in-law goes by. He is childishly afraid of ghosts and other trivialities that menace his soul, but dread of physical pain is a weakness which he is not acquainted with. He knows all the great and many of the little constellations, and has names for them; he has a symbol-writing by means of which he can convey messages far and wide among the tribes; he has a correct eye for form and expression, and draws a good picture; he can track a fugitive by delicate traces which the white man's eye cannot discern, and by methods which the finest white intelligence cannot master; he makes a missile which science itself cannot duplicate without the model—if with it; a missile whose secret baffled and defeated the searchings and theorizings of the white mathematicians for seventy years; and by an art all his own he performs miracles with it which the white man cannot approach untaught, nor parallel after teaching. Within certain limits this savage's intellect is the alertest and the brightest known to history or tradition; and yet the poor creature was never able to invent a counting system that would reach above five, nor a vessel that he could boil water in. He is the prize-curiosity of all the races. To all intents and purposes he is dead—in the body; but he has features that will live in literature.

Mr. Philip Chauncy, an officer of the Victorian Government, contributed to its archives a report of his personal observations of the aboriginals which has in it some things which I wish to condense slightly and insert here. He speaks of the quickness of their eyes and the accuracy of their judgment of the direction of approaching missiles as being quite extraordinary, and of the answering suppleness and accuracy of limb and muscle in avoiding the missile as being extraordinary also. He has seen an aboriginal stand as a target for cricket-balls thrown with great force ten or fifteen yards, by professional bowlers, and successfully dodge them or parry them with his shield during about half an hour. One of those balls, properly placed, could have killed him; 'Yet he depended, with the utmost self-possession, on the quickness of his eye and his agility.'

The shield was the customary war-shield of his race, and would not be a protection to you or to me. It is no broader than a stovepipe, and is about as long as a man's arm. The opposing surface is not flat, but slopes away from the centerline like a boat's bow. The difficulty about a cricket-ball that has been thrown with a scientific 'twist' is, that it suddenly changes its course when it is close to its target and comes straight for the mark when apparently it was going overhead or to one side. I should not be able to protect myself from such balls for half-an-hour, or less.

Mr. Chauncy once saw 'a little native man' throw a cricket-ball 119 yards. This is said to beat the English professional record by thirteen yards.

We have all seen the circus-man bound into the air from a spring-board and make a somersault over eight horses standing side by side. Mr. Chauncy saw an aboriginal do it over eleven; and was assured that he had sometimes done it over fourteen. But what is that to this:

> I saw the same man leap from the *ground*, and in going over he dipped his head, unaided by his hands, into a hat placed in an inverted position on the top of the head of another man sitting upright on horseback—both man and horse being of the

average size. The native landed on the other side of the horse with the hat fairly on his head. The prodigious height of the leap, and the precision with which it was taken so as to enable him to dip his head into the hat, exceeded any feat of the kind I have ever beheld.

I should think so! On board a ship lately I saw a young Oxford athlete *run four steps* and spring into the air and squirm his hips by a side-twist over a bar that was five and one-half feet high; but he could not have stood still and cleared a bar that was *four* feet high. I know this, because I tried it myself.

One can see now where the kangaroo learned its art.

Sir George Grey and Mr. Eyre testify that the natives dug wells fourteen or fifteen feet deep and two feet in diameter at the bore—dug them in the *sand*—wells that were 'quite circular, carried straight down, and the work beautifully executed.'

Their tools were their hands and feet. How did they throw sand out from such a depth? How could they stoop down and get it, with only two feet of space to stoop in? How did they keep that sand-pipe from caving in on them? I do not know. Still, they did manage those seeming impossibilities. Swallowed the sand, may be.

Mr. Chauncy speaks highly of the patience and skill and alert intelligence of the native huntsman when he is stalking the emu, the kangaroo, and other game:

> As he walks through the bush his step is light, elastic, and noiseless; every track on the earth catches

> his keen eye; a leaf, or fragment of a stick turned, or a blade of grass recently bent by the tread of one of the lower animals, instantly arrests his attention; in fact, nothing escapes his quick and powerful sight on the ground, in the trees, or in the distance, which may supply him with a meal or warn him of danger. A little examination of the trunk of a tree which may be nearly covered with the scratches of opossums ascending and descending is sufficient to inform him whether one *went up the night before without coming down again or not.*

Fennimore Cooper lost his chance. He would have known how to value these people. He wouldn't have traded the dullest of them for the brightest Mohawk he ever invented.

All savages draw outline pictures upon bark; but the resemblances are not close, and expression is usually lacking. But the Australian aboriginal's pictures of animals were nicely accurate in form, attitude, carriage; and he put spirit into them, and expression. And his pictures of white people and natives were pretty nearly as good as his pictures of the other animals. He dressed his whites in the fashion of their day, both the ladies and the gentlemen. As an untaught wielder of the pencil it is not likely that he has had his equal among savage people.

His place in art—as to drawing, not color-work—is well up, all things considered. His art is not to be classified with savage art at all, but on a plane two degrees above it and one degree above the lowest plane of civilized art. To be exact, his place in art is between

Botticelli and De Maurier. That is to say, he could not draw as well as De Maurier but better than Boticelli. In feeling, he resembles both; also in grouping and in his preferences in the matter of subjects. His 'corrobboree' of the Australian wilds reappears in De Maurier's Belgravian ballrooms, with clothes and the smirk of civilization added; Botticelli's 'Spring' is the corrobboree further idealized, but with fewer clothes and more smirk. And well enough as to intention, *but*—my word!

The aboriginal can make a fire by friction. I have tried that.

All savages are able to stand a good deal of physical pain. The Australian aboriginal has this quality in a well-developed degree. Do not read the following instances if horrors are not pleasant to you. They were recorded by the Rev. Henry N. Wolloston, of Melbourne, who had been a surgeon before he became a clergyman:

> 1. In the summer of 1852 I started on horseback from Albany, King George's Sound, to visit at Cape Riche, accompanied by a native on foot. We traveled about forty miles the first day, then camped by a water-hole for the night. After cooking and eating our supper, I observed the native, who had said nothing to me on the subject, collect the hot embers of the fire together, and deliberately place his right foot in the glowing mass for a moment, then suddenly withdraw it, stamping on the ground and uttering a long-drawn guttural sound of mingled pain and satisfaction. This operation he

repeated several times. On my inquiring the meaning of his strange conduct, he only said, 'Me carpenter-make 'em' ('I am mending my foot'), and then showed me his charred great toe, the nail of which had been torn off by a tea-tree stump, in which it had been caught during the journey, and the pain of which he had borne with stoical composure until the evening, when he had an opportunity of cauterizing the wound in the primitive manner above described.

And he proceeded on the journey the next day, 'as if nothing had happened'—and walked thirty miles. It was a strange idea, to keep a surgeon and then do his own surgery.

2. A native about twenty-five years of age once applied to me, as a doctor, to extract the wooden barb of a spear, which, during a fight in the bush some four months previously, had entered his chest, just missing the heart, and penetrated the viscera to a considerable depth. The spear had been cut off, leaving the barb behind, which continued to force its way by muscular action gradually toward the back; and when I examined him I could feel a hard substance between the ribs below the left blade-bone. I made a deep incision, and with a pair of forceps extracted the barb, which was made, as usual, of hard wood about four inches long and from half an inch to an inch thick. It was very smooth, and partly digested, so to speak, by the maceration to which it had been exposed during its four months' journey through the body. The wound made by the

spear had long since healed, leaving only a small cicatrix; and after the operation, which the native bore without flinching, he appeared to suffer no pain. Indeed, judging from his good state of health, the presence of the foreign matter did not materially annoy him. He was perfectly well in a few days.

But No. 3 is my favorite. Whenever I read it I seem to enjoy all that the patient enjoyed—whatever it was:

3. Once at King George's Sound a native presented himself to me with one leg only, and requested me to supply him with a wooden leg. He had traveled in this maimed state about ninety-six miles, for this purpose. I examined the limb, which had been severed just below the knee, and found that it had been charred by fire, while about two inches of the partially calcined bone protruded through the flesh. I at once removed this with the saw; and having made as presentable a stump of it as I could, covered the amputated end of the bone with a surrounding of muscle, and kept the patient a few days under my care to allow the wound to heal. On inquiring, the native told me that in a fight with other black fellows a spear had struck his leg and penetrated the bone below the knee. Finding it was serious, he had recourse to the following crude and barbarous operation, which it appears is not uncommon among these people in their native state. He made a fire, and dug a hole in the earth only sufficiently large to admit his leg, and deep enough to allow the wounded part to be on a level with the surface of the ground. He then *surrounded the limb with the live*

coals or charcoal, which was replenished until the leg was literally burnt off. The cauterization thus applied completely checked the hemorrhage, and he was able in a day or two to hobble down to the Sound, with the aid of a long stout stick, although he was more than a week on the road.

But he was a fastidious native. He soon discarded the wooden leg made for him by the doctor, because 'it had no feeling in it.' It must have had as much as the one he burnt off, I should think.

So much for the Aboriginals. It is difficult for me to let them alone. They are marvelously interesting creatures. For a quarter of a century, now, the several colonial governments have housed their remnants in comfortable stations, and fed them well and taken good care of them in every way. If I had found this out while I was in Australia I could have seen some of those people—but I didn't. I would walk thirty miles to see a stuffed one.

Australia has a slang of its own. This is a matter of course. The vast cattle and sheep industries, the strange aspects of the country, and the strange native animals, brute and human, are matters which would naturally breed a local slang. I have notes of this slang somewhere, but at the moment I can call to mind only a few of the words and phrases. They are expressive ones. The wide, sterile, unpeopled deserts have created eloquent phrases like 'No Man's Land' and the 'Never-never Country.' Also this felicitous form: 'She lives in the Never-never Country'—that is, she is an old maid. And this one is not without merit: 'heifer-paddock'—

young ladies' seminary. 'Bail up' and 'stick up' equivalent of our highwayman-term to 'hold up' a stage-coach or a train. 'New-chum' is the equivalent of our 'tenderfoot'—new arrival.

And then there is the immortal 'My word! 'We must import it. 'M-y *word*! In cold print it is the equivalent of our 'Ger-*rreat Caesar*!' but spoken with the proper Australian unction and fervency, it is worth six of it for grace and charm and expressiveness. Our form is rude and explosive; it is not suited to the drawing-room or the heifer-paddock; but 'M-y *word*!' is, and is music to the ear, too, when the utterer knows how to say it. I saw it in print several times on the Pacific Ocean, but it struck me coldly, it aroused no sympathy. That was because it was the dead corpse of the thing, the soul was not there—the tones were lacking—the informing spirit—the deep feeling—the eloquence. But the first time I heard an Australian say it, it was positively thrilling.

15

The Bird with a Forgettable Name

> Be careless in your dress if you must,
> but keep a tidy soul.
>
> —*Pudd'nhead Wilson's New Calendar*

We left Adelaide in due course, and went to Horsham, in the colony of Victoria; a good deal of a journey, if I remember rightly, but pleasant. Horsham sits in a plain which is as level as a floor—one of those famous dead levels which Australian books describe so often; gray, bare, sombre, melancholy, baked, cracked, in the tedious long drouths, but a horizonless ocean of vivid green grass the day after a rain. A country town, peaceful, reposeful, inviting, full of snug homes, with garden plots, and plenty of shrubbery and flowers.

Horsham, October 17. At the hotel. The weather divine. Across the way, in front of the London Bank of Australia, is a very handsome cottonwood. It is in opulent leaf, and every leaf perfect. The full power of the on-rushing spring is upon it, and I imagine I can see it grow. Alongside the bank and a little way back in the garden there is a row of soaring fountain-sprays of delicate feathery foliage quivering in the breeze, and mottled with flashes of light that shift and play through the mass like flash-lights through an opal—a most beautiful tree, and a striking contrast to the cottonwood. Every leaf of the cottonwood is distinctly defined—it is a kodak for faithful, hard, unsentimental detail; the other an impressionist picture, delicious to look upon, full of a subtle and exquisite charm, but all details fused in a swoon of vague and soft loveliness.

It turned out, upon inquiry, to be a pepper tree—an importation from China. It has a silky sheen, soft and rich. I saw some that had long red bunches of currant-like berries ambushed among the foliage. At a distance, in certain lights, they give the tree a pinkish tint and a new charm.

There is an agricultural college eight miles from Horsham. We were driven out to it by its chief. The conveyance was an open wagon; the time, noonday; no wind; the sky without a cloud, the sunshine brilliant—and the mercury at 92° in the shade. In some countries an indolent unsheltered drive of an hour and a half under such conditions would have been a sweltering and prostrating experience; but there was nothing of that in this case. It is a climate that is perfect. There was no sense of heat; indeed, there was no heat; the air was fine and pure and exhilarating; if the drive had lasted half a day I think we should not have felt any discomfort, or grown silent or droopy or tired. Of course, the secret of it was the exceeding dryness of the atmosphere. In that plain 112° in the shade is without doubt no harder upon a man than is 88° or 90° in New York.

The road lay through the middle of an empty space which seemed to me to be a hundred yards wide between the fences. I was not given the width in yards, but only in chains and perches—and furlongs, I think. I would have given a good deal to know what the width was, but I did not pursue the matter. I think it is best to put up with information the way you get it; and seem satisfied with it, and surprised at it, and grateful for it, and say, 'My word!' and never let on. It was a wide space; I could tell you how wide, in chains and perches and furlongs and things, but that would not help you any. Those things sound well, but they are shadowy and indefinite, like 'troy weight' and 'avoirdupois'; nobody knows what they mean. When you buy a pound of a drug and the man asks you which you want, troy or avoirdupois, it is best to say 'Yes,' and shift the subject.

They said that the wide space dates from the earliest sheep and cattle-raising days. People had to drive their stock long distances—immense journeys—from worn-out places to new ones where were water and fresh pasturage; and this wide space had to be left in grass and unfenced, or the stock would have starved to death in the transit.

On the way we saw the usual birds—the beautiful little green parrots, the magpie, and some others;

and also the slender native bird of modest plumage and the eternally-forgettable name—the bird that is the smartest among birds, and can give a parrot 30 to 1 in the game and then talk him to death. I cannot recall that bird's name. I think it begins with M. I wish it began with G. or something that a person can remember.

The magpie was out in great force, in the fields and on the fences. He is a handsome large creature, with snowy white decorations, and is a singer; he has a murmurous rich note that is lovely. He was once modest, even diffident; but he lost all that when he found out that he was Australia's sole musical bird. He has talent, and cuteness, and impudence; and in his tame state he is a most satisfactory pet—never coming when he is called, always coming when he isn't, and studying disobedience as an accomplishment. He is not confined, but loafs all over the house and grounds, like the laughing jackass. I think he learns to talk, I know he learns to sing tunes, and his friends say that he knows how to steal without learning. I was acquainted with a tame magpie in Melbourne. He had lived in a lady's house several years, and believed he owned it. The lady had tamed him, and in return he had tamed the lady. He was always on deck when not wanted, always having his own way, always tyrannizing over the dog, and always making the cat's life a slow sorrow and a martyrdom. He knew a number of tunes and could sing them in perfect time and tune; and would do it, too, at any time that silence was wanted; and then encore himself and do it again; but if he was asked to sing he would go out and take a walk.

It was long believed that fruit trees would not grow in that baked and waterless plain around Horsham, but the agricultural college has dissipated that idea. Its ample nurseries were producing oranges, apricots, lemons, almonds, peaches, cherries, 48 varieties of apples—in fact, all manner of fruits, and in abundance. The trees did not seem to miss the water; they were in vigorous and flourishing condition.

Experiments are made with different soils, to see what things thrive best in them and what climates are best for them. A man who is ignorantly trying to produce upon his farm things not suited to its soil and its other conditions can make a journey to the college from anywhere in Australia, and go back with a change of scheme which will make his farm productive and profitable.

There were forty pupils there—a few of them farmers, re-learning their trade, the rest young men mainly from the cities—novices. It seemed a strange thing that an agricultural college should have an attraction for city-bred youths, but such is the fact. They are good stuff, too; they are above the agricultural average of intelligence, and they come without any inherited prejudices in favor of hoary ignorances made sacred by long descent.

The students work all day in the fields, the nurseries, and the shearing-sheds, learning and doing all the practical work of the business—three days in a week. On the other three they study and hear lectures. They are taught the beginnings of such sciences as bear upon agriculture—like chemistry, for instance. We saw the sophomore class in sheep-shearing shear a dozen sheep. They did it by hand, not with the machine. The sheep was seized and flung down on his side and held there; and the students took off his coat with great celerity and adroitness. Sometimes they clipped off a sample of the sheep, but that is customary with shearers, and they don't mind it; they don't even mind it as much as the sheep. They dab a splotch of sheep-dip on the place and go right ahead.

The coat of wool was unbelievably thick. Before the shearing the sheep looked like the fat woman in the circus; after it he looked like a bench. He was clipped to the skin; and smoothly and uniformly. The fleece comes from him all in one piece and has the spread of a blanket.

The college was flying the Australian flag—the gridiron of England smuggled up in the northwest corner of a big red field that had the random stars of the Southern Cross wandering around over it.

From Horsham we went to Stawell. By rail. Still in the colony of Victoria. Stawell is in the gold-mining country. In the bank-safe was half a peck of surface-gold—gold dust, grain gold; rich; pure in fact, and pleasant to sift through one's fingers; and would be pleasanter if it would stick. And there were a couple of gold bricks, very heavy to handle, and worth $7,500 a piece. They were from a very valuable quartz mine; a lady owns two-thirds of it; she has an income of $75,000 a month from it, and is able to keep house.

The Stawell region is not productive of gold only; it has great vineyards, and produces exceptionally fine wines. One of these vineyards—the Great Western, owned by Mr. Irving—is regarded as a model. Its product has reputation abroad. It yields a choice champagne and a fine claret, and its hock took a prize in France two or three years ago. The champagne is kept in a maze of passages under ground, cut in the rock, to secure it an even temperature during the three-year term required to perfect it. In those vaults I saw 120,000 bottles of champagne. The colony of Victoria has a population of 1,000,000, and those people are said to drink 25,000,000 bottles of champagne per year. The dryest community on the earth. The government has lately reduced the duty upon foreign wines. That is one of the unkindnesses of Protection. A man invests years of work and a vast sum of money in a worthy enterprise, upon the faith of existing laws; then the law is changed, and the man is robbed by his own government.

On the way back to Stawell we had a chance to see a group of boulders called the Three Sisters—a curiosity oddly located; for it was upon high ground, with the land sloping away from it, and no height above it from whence the boulders could have rolled down. Relics of an early ice-drift, perhaps. They are noble boulders. One of them has the size and smoothness and plump sphericity of a balloon of the biggest pattern.

The road led through a forest of great gum-trees, lean and scraggy and sorrowful. The road was cream-white—a clayey kind of earth, apparently. Along it toiled occasional freight wagons, drawn by long double files of oxen. Those wagons were going a journey of two hundred miles, I was told, and were running a successful opposition to the railway! The railways are owned and run by the government.

Those sad gums stood up out of the dry white clay, pictures of patience and resignation. It is a tree that can get along without water; still it is fond of it—ravenously so. It is a very intelligent tree and will detect the presence of hidden water at a distance of fifty feet, and send out slender long root-fibres to prospect it. They will find it; and will also get at it—even through a cement wall six inches thick. Once a cement water-pipe under ground at Stawell began to gradually reduce its output, and finally ceased altogether to deliver water. Upon examining into the matter it was found stopped up, wadded compactly with a mass of root-fibres, delicate and hair-like. How this stuff had gotten into the pipe was a puzzle for some little time; finally it was found that it had crept in through a crack that was almost invisible to the eye. A gum tree forty feet away had tapped the pipe and was drinking the water.

16

Ballarat and the Great Nuggets

> There is no such thing as 'the Queen's English.' The property has gone into the hands of a joint stock company and we own the bulk of the shares!
>
> —*Pudd'nhead Wilson's New Calendar*

Frequently, in Australia, one has cloud-effects of an unfamiliar sort. We had this kind of scenery, finely staged, all the way to Ballarat. Consequently we saw more sky than country on that journey. At one time a great stretch of the vault was densely flecked with wee ragged-edged flakes of painfully white cloud-stuff, all of one shape and size, and equidistant apart, with narrow cracks of adorable blue showing between. The whole was suggestive of a hurricane of snow-flakes drifting across the skies. By and by these flakes fused themselves together in interminable lines, with shady faint hollows between the lines, the long satin-surfaced rollers following each other in simulated movement, and enchantingly counterfeiting the majestic march of a flowing sea. Later, the sea solidified itself; then gradually broke up its mass into innumerable lofty white pillars of about one size, and ranged these across the firmament, in receding and fading perspective, in the similitude of a stupendous colonnade—a mirage without a doubt flung from the far Gates of the Hereafter.

The approaches to Ballarat were beautiful. The features, great green expanses of rolling pasture-land, bisected by eye-contenting hedges of commingled new-gold and old-gold gorse—and a lovely lake. One must put in the pause, there, to fetch the reader up with a slight jolt, and keep him from gliding by without noticing the lake. One must notice it; for a lovely lake is not as common a thing along the railways of Australia as are the dry places. Ninety-two in the shade again, but balmy and comfortable, fresh and bracing. A perfect climate.

Forty-five years ago the site now occupied by the City of Ballarat was a sylvan solitude as quiet as Eden and as lovely. Nobody had ever heard of it. On the 25th of August, 1851, the first *great* gold-strike made in Australia was made here. The wandering prospectors who made it scraped up two pounds and a half of gold the first day—worth $600. A few days later the place was a hive—a town. The news of the strike spread everywhere in a sort of instantaneous way—spread like a flash to the very ends of the earth. A celebrity so prompt and so universal has hardly been paralleled in history, perhaps. It was as if the name BALLARAT had suddenly been written on the sky, where all the world could read it at once.

The smaller discoveries made in the colony of New South Wales three months before had already started emigrants toward Australia; they had been coming as a stream, but they came as a flood, now. A hundred thousand people poured into Melbourne from England and other countries in a single month, and flocked away to the mines. The crews of the ships that brought them flocked with them; the clerks in the government offices followed; so did the cooks, the maids, the coachmen, the butlers, and the other domestic servants; so did the carpenters, the smiths, the plumbers, the painters, the reporters, the editors, the lawyers, the clients, the barkeepers, the bummers, the blacklegs, the thieves, the loose women, the grocers, the butchers, the bakers, the doctors, the druggists, the nurses; so did the police; even officials of high and hitherto envied place threw up their positions and joined the procession. This roaring avalanche swept out of Melbourne and left it desolate, Sunday-like, paralyzed, everything at a stand-still, the ships lying idle at anchor, all signs of life departed, all sounds stilled save the rasping of the cloud-shadows as they scraped across the vacant streets.

That grassy and leafy paradise at Ballarat was soon ripped open, and lacerated and scarified and gutted, in the feverish search for its hidden riches. There is nothing like surface-mining to snatch the graces and beauties and benignities out of a paradise, and make an odious and repulsive spectacle of it.

What fortunes were made! Immigrants got rich while the ship unloaded and reloaded—and went back home for good in the same cabin they had come out in! Not all of them. Only some. I saw the others in Ballarat myself, forty-five years later—what were left of them by time and death and the disposition to rove. They were young and gay, then; they are patriarchal and grave, now; and they do not get excited any more. They talk of the Past. They live in it. Their life is a dream, a retrospection.

Ballarat was a great region for 'nuggets.' No such nuggets were found in California as Ballarat produced. In fact, the Ballarat region has yielded the largest ones known to history. Two of them weighed about 180 pounds each, and together were worth $90,000. They were offered to any poor person who would shoulder them and carry them away. Gold was so plentiful that it made people liberal like that.

Ballarat was a swarming city of tents in the early days. Everybody was happy, for a time, and apparently prosperous. Then came trouble. The government swooped down with a mining tax. And in its worst form, too; for it was not a tax upon what the miner had taken out, but upon what he was *going* to take out—if he could find it. It was a license—tax license to work his claim—and it had to be paid before he could begin digging.

Consider the situation. No business is so uncertain as surface-mining. Your claim may be good, and it may be worthless. It may make you well off in a month; and then again you may have to dig and slave for half a year, at heavy expense, only to find out at last that the gold is not there in cost-paying quantity, and that your time and your hard work have been thrown away. It might be wise policy to advance the miner a monthly sum to encourage him to develop the country's riches; but to tax him monthly in advance instead—why, such a thing was never dreamed of in America. There, neither the claim itself nor its products, howsoever rich or poor, were taxed.

The Ballarat miners protested, petitioned, complained—it was of no use; the government held its ground, and went on collecting the tax. And not by pleasant methods, but by ways which must have been very galling to free people. The rumblings of a coming storm began to be audible.

By and by there was a result; and I think it may be called the finest thing in Australasian history. It was a revolution—small in size, but great politically; it was a strike for liberty, a struggle for a principle, a stand against injustice and oppression. It was the Barons and John, over again; it was Hampden and Ship-Money; it was Concord and Lexington; small beginnings, all of them, but all of them great in political results, all of them epoch-making. It is another instance of a victory won by a lost battle. It adds an honorable page to history; the people know it and are proud of it. They keep green the memory of the men who fell at the Eureka Stockade, and Peter Lalor has his monument.

The surface-soil of Ballarat was full of gold. This soil the miners ripped and tore and trenched and harried and disemboweled, and made it yield up its immense treasure. Then they went down into the earth with deep shafts, seeking the gravelly beds of ancient rivers and brooks—and found them. They followed the courses of these streams, and gutted them, sending the gravel up in buckets to the upper world, and washing out of it its enormous deposits of gold. The next biggest of the two monster nuggets mentioned above came from an old river-channel 180 feet under ground.

Finally the quartz lodes were attacked. That is not poor-man's mining. Quartz-mining and milling require capital, and staying-power, and patience. Big companies were formed, and for several decades, now, the lodes have been successfully worked, and have yielded great wealth. Since the gold discovery in 1853 the Ballarat mines—taking the three kinds of mining together—have contributed to the world's pocket something over *three hundred millions of dollars*, which is to say that this nearly invisible little spot on the earth's surface has yielded about one-fourth as much gold in forty-four years as all California has yielded in forty-seven. The Californian aggregate, from 1848 to 1895, inclusive, as reported by the Statistician of the United States Mint, is $1,265,217,217.

A citizen told me a curious thing about those mines. With all my experience of mining I had never heard of anything of the sort before. The main gold reef runs about north and south—of course—for that is the custom of a rich gold reef. At Ballarat its course is between walls of slate. Now the citizen told me that throughout a stretch of twelve miles along the reef, the reef is crossed at intervals by a straight black streak of a carbonaceous nature—a streak in the slate; a streak no thicker than a pencil—and that wherever it crosses the reef you will certainly find gold at the junction. It is called the Indicator. Thirty feet on each side of the Indicator (and down in the slate, of course) is a still finer streak—a streak as fine as a pencil mark; and indeed, that is its name—Pencil Mark. Whenever you find the Pencil Mark you know that thirty feet from it is the Indicator; you measure the distance, excavate, find the Indicator, trace it straight to the reef, and sink your shaft; your fortune is made, for certain. If that is true, it is curious. And it is curious anyway.

Ballarat is a town of only 40,000 population; and yet, since it is in Australia, it has every essential of an advanced and enlightened big city. This is pure matter of course. I must stop dwelling upon these things. It is hard to keep from dwelling upon them, though; for it is difficult to get away from the surprise of it. I will let the other details go, this time, but I must allow myself to mention that this little town has a park of 326 acres; a flower garden of 83 acres, with an elaborate and expensive fernery in it and some costly and unusually fine statuary; and an artificial lake covering 600 acres, equipped with a fleet of 200 shells, small sail boats, and little steam yachts.

At this point I strike out some other praiseful things which I was tempted to add. I do not strike them out because they were not true or not well said, but because I find them better said by another man—and a man more competent to testify, too, because he belongs on the ground, and knows. I clip them from a chatty speech delivered some years ago by Mr. William Little, who was at that time mayor of Ballarat:

The language of our citizens, in this as in other parts of Australasia, is mostly healthy Anglo-Saxon, free from Americanisms, vulgarisms, and the conflicting dialects of our Fatherland, and is pure enough to suit a Trench or a Latham. Our youth, aided by climatic influence, are in point of physique and comeliness unsurpassed in the Sunny South. Our young men are well ordered; and our maidens, 'not stepping over the bounds of modesty,' are as fair as Psyches, dispensing smiles as charming as November flowers.

The closing clause has the seeming of a rather frosty compliment, but that is apparent only, not real. November is summer-time there.

His compliment to the local purity of the language is warranted. It is quite free from impurities; this is acknowledged far and wide. As in the German Empire all cultivated people claim to speak Hanovarian German, so in Australasia all cultivated people claim to speak Ballarat English. Even in England this cult has made considerable progress, and now that it is favored by the two great Universities, the time is not far away when Ballarat English will come into general use among the educated classes of Great Britain at large. Its great merit is, that it is shorter than ordinary English—that is, it is more compressed. At first you have some difficulty in understanding it when it is spoken as rapidly as the orator whom I have quoted speaks it. An illustration will show what I mean. When he called and I handed him a chair, he bowed and said 'Q.' Presently, when we were lighting our cigars, he held a match to mine and I said 'Thank you,' and he said: 'Km.'

Then I saw. Q is the end of the phrase 'I thank you' Km is the end of the phrase 'You are welcome.' Mr. Little puts no emphasis upon either of them, but delivers them so reduced that they hardly have a sound. All Ballarat English is like that, and the effect is very soft and pleasant; it takes all the hardness and harshness out of our tongue and gives to it a delicate whispery and vanishing cadence which charms the ear like the faint rustling of the forest leaves.

17

The Mark Twain Club

'Classic.' A book which people praise and don't read.

—*Pudd'nhead Wilson's New Calendar*

On the rail again—bound for Bendigo. From diary:

October 23. Got up at 6, left at 7.30; soon reached Castlemaine, one of the rich gold-fields of the early days; waited several hours for a train; left at 3.40 and reached Bendigo in an hour. For comrade, a Catholic priest who was better than I was, but didn't seem to know it—a man full of graces of the heart, the mind, and the spirit; a lovable man. He will rise. He will be a bishop some day. Later an Archbishop. Later a Cardinal. Finally an Archangel, I hope. And then he will recall me when I say, 'Do you remember that trip we made from Ballarat to Bendigo, when you were nothing but Father C., and I was nothing to what I am now?'

It has actually taken nine hours to come from Ballarat to Bendigo. We could have saved seven by walking. However, there was no hurry.

Bendigo was another of the rich strikes of the early days. It does a great quartz-mining business, now—that business which, more than any other that I know of, teaches patience, and requires grit and a steady nerve. The town is full of towering chimney-stacks, and hoisting-works, and looks like a petroleum-city. Speaking of patience; for example, one of the local companies went steadily on with its deep borings and searchings without show of gold or a penny of reward for *eleven* years—then struck it, and became suddenly rich. The eleven years' work had cost $55,000, and the first gold found was a grain the size of a pin's head. It is kept under locks and bars, as a precious thing, and is reverently shown to the visitor, 'hats off.' When I saw it I had not heard its history.

> 'It is gold. Examine it—take the glass. Now how much should you say it is worth?'

I said—

> 'I should say about two cents; or in your English dialect, four farthings.'
> 'Well, it cost £11,000.'
> 'Oh, come!'
> 'Yes, it did. Ballarat and Bendigo have produced the three monumental nuggets of the world, and this one is the monumentalest one of the three. The other two represent £9,000 a piece; this one a couple of thousand more. It is small, and not much

to look at, but it is entitled to its name—Adam. It is the Adam-nugget of this mine, and its children run up into the millions.'

Speaking of patience again, another of the mines was worked, under heavy expenses, during 17 years before pay was struck, and still another one compelled a wait of 21 years before pay was struck; then, in both instances, the outlay was all back in a year or two, with compound interest.

Bendigo has turned out even more gold than Ballarat. The two together have produced $650,000,000 worth—which is half as much as California has produced.

It was through Mr. Blank—not to go into particulars about his name—it was mainly through Mr. Blank that my stay in Bendigo was made memorably pleasant and interesting. He explained this to me himself. He told me that it was through his influence that the city government invited me to the town-hall to hear complimentary speeches and respond to them; that it was through his influence that I had been taken on a long pleasure-drive through the city and shown its notable features; that it was through his influence that I was invited to visit the great mines; that it was through his influence that I was taken to the hospital and allowed to see the convalescent Chinaman who had been attacked at midnight in his lonely hut eight weeks before by robbers, and stabbed forty-six times and scalped besides; that it was through his influence that when I arrived this awful spectacle of piecings and patchings and ban-dagings was sitting up in his cot letting on to read one of my books; that it was through his influence that efforts had been made to get the Catholic Archbishop of Bendigo to invite me to dinner; that it was through his influence that efforts had been made to get the Anglican Bishop of Bendigo to ask me to supper; that it was through his influence that the dean of the editorial fraternity had driven me through the woodsy outlying country and shown me, from the summit of Lone Tree Hill, the mightiest and loveliest expanse of forest-clad mountain and valley that I had seen in all Australia. And when he asked me what had most impressed me in Bendigo and I answered and said it was the taste and the public spirit which had adorned the streets with 105 miles of shade trees, he said that it was through his influence that it had been done.

But I am not representing him quite correctly. He did not *say* it was through his influence that all these things had happened—for that would have been coarse; he merely *conveyed* that idea; conveyed it so subtly that I only caught it fleetingly, as one catches vagrant faint breaths of perfume when one traverses the meadows in summer; conveyed it without offense and without any suggestion of egoism or ostentation—but *conveyed* it, nevertheless.

He was an Irishman; an educated gentleman; grave, and kindly, and courteous; a bachelor, and about forty-five or possibly fifty years old, apparently. He called upon me at the hotel, and it was there that we had this talk. He made me like him, and did it without trouble. This was partly through his winning and gentle ways, but mainly through the amazing familiarity with

The Mark Twain Club

my books which his conversation showed. He was down to date with them, too; and if he had made them the study of his life he could hardly have been better posted as to their contents than he was. He made me better satisfied with myself than I had ever been before. It was plain that he had a deep fondness for humor, yet he never laughed; he never even chuckled; in fact, humor could not win to outward expression on his face at all. No, he was always grave—tenderly, pensively grave; but he made *me* laugh, all along; and this was very trying—and very pleasant at the same time—for it was at quotations from my own books.

When he was going, he turned and said—

> 'You don't remember me?'
> 'I? Why, no. Have we met before?'
> 'No, it was a matter of correspondence.'
> 'Correspondence?'
> 'Yes, many years ago. Twelve or fifteen. Oh, longer than that. But of course you—'

Amusing pause. Then he said—

> 'Do you remember Corrigan Castle?'
> 'N—no, I believe I don't. I don't seem to recall the name.'

He waited a moment, pondering, with the doorknob in his hand, then started out; but turned back and said that I had once been interested in Corrigan Castle, and asked me if I would go with him to his quarters in the evening and take a hot Scotch and talk it over. I was a teetotaler and liked relaxation, so I said I would.

We drove from the lecture-hall together about half-past ten. He had a most comfortably and tastefully furnished parlor, with good pictures on the walls, Indian and Japanese ornaments on the mantel, and here and there, and books everywhere—largely mine; which made me proud. The light was brilliant, the easy chairs were deep-cushioned, the arrangements for brewing and smoking were all there. We brewed and lit up; then he passed a sheet of note-paper to me and said—

'Do you remember that?'
'Oh, yes, indeed!'

The paper was of a sumptuous quality. At the top was a twisted and interlaced monogram printed from steel dies in gold and blue and red, in the ornate English fashion of long years ago; and under it, in neat gothic capitals was this—printed in blue:

THE MARK TWAIN CLUB
CORRIGAN CASTLE
...187..

'My!' said I, 'how did you come by this?'
'I was President of it.'
'No!—you don't mean it.'
'It is true. I was its first President. I was re-elected annually as long as its meetings were held in my castle—Corrigan—which was five years.'

Then he showed me an album with twenty-three photographs of me in it. Five of them were of old dates, the others of various later crops; the list closed with a picture taken by Falk in Sydney a month before.

'You sent us the first five; the rest were bought.'

This was paradise! We ran late, and talked, talked, talked—subject, the Mark Twain Club of Corrigan Castle, Ireland.

My first knowledge of that Club dates way back; all of twenty years, I should say. It came to me in the form of a courteous letter, written on the note-paper which I have described, and signed 'By order of the President; C. PEMBROKE, SECRETARY.' It conveyed the fact that the Club had been created in my honor, and added the hope that this token of appreciation of my work would meet with my approval.

I answered, with thanks; and did what I could to keep my gratification from over-exposure.

It was then that the long correspondence began. A letter came back, by order of the President, furnishing me the names of the members—thirty-two in number. With it came a copy of the Constitution and By-Laws, in pamphlet form, and artistically printed. The initiation fee and dues were in their proper place; also, schedule of meetings—monthly—for essays upon works of mine, followed by discussions; quarterly for business and a supper, without essays, but with after-supper speeches also, there was a list of the officers: President, Vice-President, Secretary, Treasurer, etc. The letter was brief, but it was pleasant reading, for it told me about the strong interest which the membership took in their new venture, etc., etc. It also asked me for a photograph—a special one. I went down and sat for it and sent it—with a letter, of course.

Presently came the badge of the Club, and very dainty and pretty it was; and very artistic. It was a frog peeping out from a graceful tangle of grass-sprays and rushes, and was done in enamels on a gold basis, and had a gold pin back of it. After I had petted it, and played with it, and caressed it, and enjoyed it a couple of hours, the light happened to fall upon it at a new angle, and revealed to me a cunning new detail; with the light just right, certain delicate shadings of the grass-blades and rush-stems wove themselves into a monogram—mine! You can see that that jewel was a work of art. And when you come to consider the intrinsic value of it, you must concede that it is not every literary club that could afford a badge like that. It was easily worth $75, in the opinion of Messrs. Marcus and Ward of New York. They said they could not duplicate it for that and make a profit.

By this time the Club was well under way; and from that time forth its secretary kept my off-hours well supplied with business. He reported the Club's discussions of my books with laborious fullness, and did his work with great spirit and ability. As a rule, he synopsized; but when a speech was especially brilliant, he short-handed it and gave me the best passages from it, written out. There were five speakers whom he particularly favored in that way: Palmer, Forbes, Naylor, Norris, and Calder. Palmer and Forbes could never get through a speech without attacking each other, and each in his own way was formidably effective—Palmer in virile and eloquent abuse, Forbes in courtly and elegant but scalding satire. I could always tell which of them was talking without looking for his name.

The Mark Twain Club

Naylor had a polished style and a happy knack at felicitous metaphor; Norris's style was wholly without ornament, but enviably compact, lucid, and strong. But after all, Calder was the gem. He never spoke when sober, he spoke continuously when he wasn't. And certainly they were the drunkest speeches that a man ever uttered. They were full of good things, but so incredibly mixed up and wandering that it made one's head swim to follow him. They were not intended to be funny, but they were—funny for the very gravity which the speaker put into his flowing miracles of incongruity. In the course of five years I came to know the styles of the five orators as well as I knew the style of any speaker in my own club at home.

These reports came every month. They were written on foolscap, 600 words to the page, and usually about twenty-five pages in a report—a good 15,000 words, I should say,—a solid week's work. The reports were absorbingly entertaining, long as they were; but, unfortunately for me, they did not come alone. They were always accompanied by a lot of questions about passages and purposes in my books, which the Club wanted answered; and additionally accompanied every quarter by the Treasurer's report, and the Auditor's report, and the Committee's report, and the President's review, and my opinion of these was always desired; also suggestions for the good of the Club, if any occurred to me.

By and by I came to dread those things; and this dread grew and grew and grew; grew until I got to anticipating them with a cold horror. For I was an indolent man, and not fond of letter-writing, and whenever these things came I had to put everything by and sit down—for my own peace of mind—and dig and dig until I got something out of my head which would answer for a reply. I got along fairly well the first year; but for the succeeding four years the Mark Twain Club of Corrigan Castle was my curse, my nightmare, the grief and misery of my life. And I got so, *so* sick of sitting for photographs. I sat every year for five years, trying to satisfy that insatiable organization. Then at last I rose in revolt. I could endure my oppressions no longer. I pulled my fortitude together and tore off my chains, and was a free man again, and happy. From that day I burned the secretary's fat envelopes the moment they arrived, and by and by they ceased to come.

Well, in the sociable frankness of that night in Bendigo I brought this all out in full confession. Then Mr. Blank came out in the same frank way, and with a preliminary word of gentle apology said that *he* was the Mark Twain Club, and the only member it had ever had!

Why, it was matter for anger, but I didn't feel any. He said he never had to work for a living, and that by the time he was thirty life had become a bore and a weariness to him. He had no interests left; they had paled and perished, one by one, and left him desolate. He had begun to think of suicide. Then all of a sudden he thought of that happy idea of starting an imaginary club, and went straightway to work at it, with enthusiasm and love. He was charmed with it; it gave him something to do. It elaborated itself on his hands; it became twenty times more complex and formidable than was his first rude draft of it. Every new addition to his original plan which cropped up in his mind gave him a fresh interest and a new pleasure. He designed the Club badge himself, and worked over it, altering and improving it, a number of days and nights; then sent to London and had it made. It was the only one that was made. It was made for me; the 'rest of the Club' went without.

He invented the thirty-two members and their names. He invented the five favorite speakers and their five separate styles. He invented their speeches, and reported them himself. He would have kept that Club going until now, if I hadn't deserted, he said. He said he worked like a slave over those reports; each of them cost him from a week to a fortnight's work, and the work gave him pleasure and kept him alive and willing to be alive. It was a bitter blow to him when the Club died.

Finally, there wasn't any Corrigan Castle. He had invented that, too.

It was wonderful—the whole thing; and altogether the most ingenious and laborious and cheerful and painstaking practical joke I have ever heard of. And I liked it; liked to hear him tell about it; yet I have been a hater of practical jokes from as long back as I can remember. Finally he said—

> 'Do you remember a note from Melbourne fourteen or fifteen years ago, telling about your lecture tour in Australia, and your death and burial in Melbourne?—a note from Henry Bascomb, of Bascomb Hall, Upper Holywell Hants.'

'Yes.'

'I wrote it.'

'M-y—word!'

'Yes, I did it. I don't know why. I just took the notion, and carried it out without stopping to think. It was wrong. It could have done harm. I was always sorry about it afterward. You must forgive me. I was Mr. Bascom's guest on his yacht, on his voyage around the world. He often spoke of you, and of the pleasant times you had had together in his home; and the notion took me, there in Melbourne, and I imitated his hand, and wrote the letter.'

So the mystery was cleared up, after so many, many years.

18

The Conciliator

> Man is the Only Animal that Blushes.
> Or needs to.
>
> —*Pudd'nhead Wilson's New Calendar*

> The universal brotherhood of man
> is our most precious possession, what
> there is of it.
>
> —*Pudd'nhead Wilson's New Calendar*

From diary:

November 1—*noon*. A fine day, a brilliant sun. Warm in the sun, cold in the shade—an icy breeze blowing out of the south. A solemn long swell rolling up northward. It comes from the South Pole, with nothing in the way to obstruct its march and tone its energy down. I have read somewhere that an acute observer among the early explorers—Cook? or Tasman?—accepted this majestic swell as trustworthy circumstantial evidence that no important land lay to the southward, and so did not waste time on a useless quest in that direction, but changed his course and went searching elsewhere.

Afternoon. Passing between Tasmania (formerly Van Diemen's Land) and neighboring islands—islands whence the poor exiled Tasmanian savages used to gaze at their lost homeland and cry; and die of broken hearts. How glad I am that all these native races are dead and gone, or nearly so. The work was mercifully swift and horrible in some portions of Australia. As far as Tasmania is concerned, the extermination was complete: not a native is left. It was a strife of years, and decades of years. The Whites and the Blacks hunted each other, ambushed each other, butchered each other. The Blacks were not numerous. But they were wary, alert, cunning, and they knew their country well. They lasted a long time, few as they were, and inflicted much slaughter upon the Whites.

The Government wanted to save the Blacks from ultimate extermination, if possible. One of its schemes was to capture them and coop them up, on a neighboring island, under guard. Bodies of Whites volunteered for the hunt, for the pay was good—£5 for each Black captured and delivered, but the success achieved was not very satisfactory. The Black was naked, and his body was greased. It was hard to get a grip on him that would hold. The Whites moved about in armed bodies, and surprised little families of natives, and did make captures; but it was suspected that in these surprises half a dozen natives were killed to one caught—and that was not what the Government desired.

Another scheme was to drive the natives into a corner of the island and fence them in by a cordon of men placed in line across the country; but the natives managed to slip through, constantly, and continue their murders and arsons.

The governor warned these unlettered savages *by printed proclamation* that they must stay in the desolate region officially appointed for them! The proclamation was a dead letter; the savages could not read it. Afterward a *picture*-proclamation was issued. It was painted up on boards, and these were nailed to trees in the forest ... Substantially it means:

1. The Governor wishes the Whites and the Blacks to love each other;
2. He loves his black subjects;
3. Blacks who kill Whites will be hanged;
4. Whites who kill Blacks will be hanged.

Upon its several schemes the Government spent £30,000 and employed the labors and ingenuities of several thousand Whites for a long time—with failure as a result. Then, at last, a quarter of a century after the beginning of the troubles between the two races, the right man was found. No, he found himself. This was George Augustus Robinson, called in history 'The Conciliator.' He was not educated, and not conspicuous in any way. He was a working bricklayer, in Hobart Town. But he must have been an amazing personality; a man worth traveling far to see. It may be his counterpart appears in history, but I do not know where to look for it.

He set himself this incredible task: to go out into the wilderness, the jungle, and the mountain-retreats where the hunted and implacable savages were hidden, and appear among them unarmed, speak the language of love and of kindness to them, and persuade them to forsake their homes and the wild free life that was so dear to them, and go with him and surrender to the hated Whites and live under their watch and ward, and upon their charity the rest of their lives! On its face it was the dream of a madman.

In the beginning, his moral-suasion project was sarcastically dubbed the *sugar plum speculation*. If the scheme was striking, and new to the world's experience, the situation was not less so. It was this. The White population numbered 40,000 in 1831; the Black population numbered *three hundred*. Not 300 warriors, but 300 men, women, and children. The Whites were armed with guns, the Blacks with clubs and spears. The Whites had fought the Blacks for a quarter of a century, and had tried every thinkable way to capture, kill, or subdue them; and could not do it. If white men of any race *could* have done it, these would have accomplished it. But every scheme had failed, the splendid 300, the matchless 300 were unconquered, and manifestly unconquerable. They would not yield, they would listen to no terms, they would fight to the bitter end. Yet they had no poet to keep up their heart, and sing the marvel of their magnificent patriotism.

At the end of five-and-twenty years of hard fighting, the surviving 300 naked patriots were still defiant, still persistent, still efficacious with their rude weapons, and the Governor and the 40,000 knew not which way to turn, nor what to do.

Then the Bricklayer—that wonderful man—proposed to go out into the wilderness, with no weapon but his tongue, and no protection but his honest eye and his humane heart; and track those embittered savages to their lairs in the gloomy forests and among the mountain snows. Naturally, he was considered a crank. But he was not quite that. In fact, he was a good way short of that. He was building upon his long and intimate knowledge of the native character. The deriders of his project were right—from their standpoint—for they believed the natives to be mere wild beasts; and Robinson was right, from his standpoint—for he believed the natives to be human beings. The truth did really lie between the two. The event proved that Robinson's judgment was soundest; but about once a month for four years the event came near to giving the verdict to the deriders, for about that frequently Robinson barely escaped falling under the native spears.

But history shows that he had a thinking head, and was not a mere wild sentimentalist. For instance, he wanted the war parties called in before he started unarmed upon his mission of peace. He wanted the best chance of success—not a half-chance. And he was very willing to have help; and so, high rewards were advertised, for any who would go unarmed with him. This opportunity was declined. Robinson persuaded some tamed natives of both sexes to go with him—a strong evidence of his persuasive powers, for those natives well knew that their destruction would be almost certain. As it turned out, they had to face death over and over again.

Robinson and his little party had a difficult undertaking upon their hands. They could not ride off, horseback, comfortably into the woods and call Leonidas and his 300 together for a talk and a treaty the following day; for the wild men were not in a body; they were scattered, immense distances apart, over regions so desolate that even the birds could not make a living with the chances offered—scattered in groups of twenty, a dozen, half a dozen, even in groups of three. And the mission must go on foot. Mr. Bonwick furnishes a description of those horrible regions, whereby it will be seen that even fugitive gangs of the hardiest and choicest human devils the world has seen—the convicts set apart to people the 'Hell of Macquarrie Harbor Station'—were never able, but once, to survive the horrors of a march through them, but starving and struggling, and fainting and failing, ate each other, and died:

> Onward, still onward, was the order of the indomitable Robinson. No one ignorant of the western country of Tasmania can form a correct idea of the traveling difficulties. While I was resident in Hobart Town, the Governor, Sir John Franklin, and his lady, undertook the western journey to Macquarrie Harbor, and suffered terribly. One man who assisted to carry her ladyship through the swamps, gave me his bitter experience of its miseries. Several were disabled for life. No wonder that but one party, escaping from Macquarrie Harbor

convict settlement, arrived at the civilized region in safety. Men perished in the scrub, were lost in snow, or were devoured by their companions. This was the territory traversed by Mr. Robinson and his Black guides. All honor to his intrepidity, and their wonderful fidelity! When they had, in the depth of winter, to cross deep and rapid rivers, pass among mountains six thousand feet high, pierce dangerous thickets, and find food in a country forsaken even by birds, we can realize their hardships.

After a frightful journey by Cradle Mountain, and over the lofty plateau of Middlesex Plains, the travelers experienced unwonted misery, and the circumstances called forth the best qualities of the noble little band. Mr. Robinson wrote afterwards to Mr. Secretary Burnett some details of this passage of horrors. In that letter, of Oct 2, 1834, he states that his Natives were very reluctant to go over the dreadful mountain passes; that 'for seven successive days we continued traveling over one solid body of snow;' that 'the snows were of incredible depth;' that 'the Natives were frequently up to their middle in snow'. But still the ill-clad, ill-fed, diseased, and way worn men and women were sustained by the cheerful voice of their unconquerable friend, and responded most nobly to his call.

Mr. Bonwick says that Robinson's friendly capture of the Big River tribe—remember, it was a whole tribe—'was by far the grandest feature of the war, and the crowning glory of his efforts.' The word 'war' was not well chosen, and is misleading. There *was* war still, but only the Blacks were conducting it—the Whites were holding off until Robinson could give his scheme a fair trial. I think that we are to understand that the friendly capture of that tribe was by far the most important thing, the highest in value, that happened during the whole thirty years of truceless hostilities; that it was a decisive thing, a peaceful Waterloo, the surrender of the native Napoleon and his dreaded forces, the happy ending of the long strife. For 'that tribe was the terror of the colony,' its chief 'the Black Douglas of Bush households.'

Robinson knew that these formidable people were lurking somewhere, in some remote corner of the hideous regions just described, and he and his unarmed little party started on a tedious and perilous hunt for them. At last, 'there, under the shadows of the Frenchman's Cap, whose grim cone rose five thousand feet in the uninhabited westward interior' they were found. It was a serious moment. Robinson himself believed, for once, that his mission, successful until now, was to end here in failure, and that his own death-hour had struck.

The redoubtable chief stood in menacing attitude, with his eighteen-foot spear poised; his warriors stood massed at his back, armed for battle, their faces eloquent with their long-cherished loathing for white men. 'They rattled their spears and shouted their war-cry.' Their women were back of them, laden with supplies of weapons, and keeping their 150 eager dogs quiet until the chief should give the signal to fall on.

'I think we shall soon be in the resurrection,' whispered a member of Robinson's little party.

'I think we shall,' answered Robinson; then plucked up heart and began his persuasions—in the tribe's own dialect, which surprised and pleased the chief. Presently there was an interruption by the chief:

> 'Who are you?'
> 'We are gentlemen.'
> 'Where are your guns?'
> 'We have none.'

The warrior was astonished.

> 'Where your little guns?' (pistols).
> 'We have none.'

A few minutes passed—in by-play—suspense—discussion among the tribesmen—Robinson's tamed squaws ventured to cross the line and begin persuasions upon the wild squaws. Then the chief stepped back 'to confer with the old women—the real arbiters of savage war.' Mr. Bonwick continues:

> As the fallen gladiator in the arena looks for the signal of life or death from the president of the amphitheatre, so waited our friends in anxious suspense while the conference continued. In a few minutes, before a word was uttered, the women of the tribe threw up their arms three times. This was the inviolable sign of peace! Down fell the spears. Forward, with a heavy sigh of relief, and upward glance of gratitude, came the friends of peace. The impulsive natives rushed forth with tears and cries, as each saw in the other's rank a loved one of the past...

> It was a jubilee of joy. A festival followed. And, while tears flowed at the recital of woe, a corrobory [sic] of pleasant laughter closed the eventful day.

In four years, without the spilling of a drop of blood, Robinson brought them all in, willing captives, and delivered them to the white governor, and ended the war which powder and bullets, and thousands of men to use them, had prosecuted without result since 1804.

Marsyas charming the wild beasts with his music—that is fable; but the miracle wrought by Robinson is fact. It is history—and authentic; and surely, there is nothing greater, nothing more reverence-compelling in the history of any country, ancient or modern.

And in memory of the greatest man Australasia ever developed or ever will develop, there is a stately monument to George Augustus Robinson, the Conciliator in—no, it is to another man, I forget his name.

However, Robertson's own generation honored him, and in manifesting it honored themselves. The Government gave him a money-reward and a thousand acres of land; and the people held mass-meetings and praised him and emphasized their praise with a large subscription of money.

A good dramatic situation; but the curtain fell on another:

> When this desperate tribe was thus captured, there was much surprise to find that the £30,000 of a little earlier day had been spent, and the whole population of the colony placed under arms, in contention with an opposing force of *sixteen men with*

wooden spears! Yet such was the fact. The celebrated Big River tribe, that had been raised by European fears to a host, consisted of *sixteen men, nine women, and one child*. With a knowledge of the mischief done by these few, their wonderful marches and their widespread aggressions, their enemies cannot deny to them the attributes of courage and military tact. A Wallace might harass a large army with a small and determined band; but the contending parties were at least equal in arms and civilization. The Zulus who fought us in Africa, the Maories in New Zealand, the Arabs in the Soudan, were far better provided with weapons, more advanced in the science of war, and considerably more numerous, than the naked Tasmanians. Governor Arthur rightly termed them a *noble race*.

These were indeed wonderful people, the natives. They ought not to have been wasted. They should have been crossed with the Whites. It would have improved the Whites and done the Natives no harm.

But the Natives *were* wasted, poor heroic wild creatures. They were gathered together in little settlements on neighboring islands, and paternally cared for by the Government, and instructed in religion, and deprived of tobacco, because the superintendent of the Sunday-school was not a smoker, and so considered smoking immoral.

The Natives were not used to clothes, and houses, and regular hours, and church, and school, and Sunday-school, and work, and the other misplaced persecutions of civilization, and they pined for their lost home and their wild free life. Too late they repented that they had traded that heaven for this hell. They sat homesick on their alien crags, and day by day gazed out through their tears over the sea with unappeasable longing toward the hazy bulk which was the specter of what had been their paradise; one by one their hearts broke and they died.

In a very few years nothing but a scant remnant remained alive. A handful lingered along into age. In 1864 the last man died, in 1876 the last woman died, and the Spartans of Australasia were extinct.

The Whites always mean well when they take human fish out of the ocean and try to make them dry and warm and happy and comfortable in a chicken coop; but the kindest-hearted white man can always be depended on to prove himself inadequate when he deals with savages. He cannot turn the situation around and imagine how he would like it to have a well-meaning savage transfer him from his house and his church and his clothes and his Books and his choice food to a hideous wilderness of sand and rocks and snow, and ice and sleet and storm and blistering sun, with no shelter, no bed, no covering for his and his family's naked bodies, and nothing to eat but snakes and grubs and offal. This would be a hell to him; and if he had any wisdom he would know that his own civilization is a hell to the savage—but he hasn't any, and has never had any; and for lack of it he shut up those poor natives in the unimaginable perdition of his civilization, committing his crime with the very best intentions, and saw those poor creatures waste away under his tortures; and gazed at it, vaguely troubled and sorrowful, and wondered what could be the matter with them. One is almost betrayed into respecting those criminals, they were so sincerely kind, and tender, and humane, and well-meaning.

They didn't know why those exiled savages faded away, and they did their honest best to reason it out. And one man, in a like case in New South Wales, *did* reason it out and arrive at a solution:

> It is from the wrath of God, which is revealed from heaven against all ungodliness and unrighteousness of men.

> That settles it.

19

When the Moment Comes the Man Appears

Let us be thankful for the fools. But for them the rest of us could not succeed.

—*Pudd'nhead Wilson's New Calendar*

The aphorism does really seem true: 'Given the Circumstances, the Man will appear.' But the man musn't appear ahead of time, or it will spoil everything. In Robinson's case the Moment had been approaching for a quarter of a century—and meantime the future Conciliator was tranquilly laying bricks in Hobart. When all other means had failed, the Moment had arrived, and the Bricklayer put down his trowel and came forward. Earlier he would have been jeered back to his trowel again. It reminds me of a tale that was told me by a Kentuckian on the train when we were crossing Montana. He said the tale was current in Louisville years ago. He thought it had been in print, but could not remember. At any rate, in substance it was this, as nearly as I can call it back to mind.

A few years before the outbreak of the Civil War it began to appear that Memphis, Tennessee, was going to be a great tobacco *entrepot*—the wise could see the signs of it. At that time Memphis had a wharfboat, of course. There was a paved sloping wharf, for the accommodation of freight, but the steamers landed on the outside of the wharfboat, and all loading and unloading was done across it, between steamer and shore. A number of wharfboat clerks were needed, and part of the time, every day, they were very busy, and part of the time tediously idle. They were boiling over with youth and spirits, and they had to make the intervals of idleness endurable in some way; and as a rule, they did it by contriving practical jokes and playing them upon each other.

The favorite butt for the jokes was Ed Jackson, because he played none himself, and was easy game for other people's—for he always believed whatever was told him.

One day he told the others his scheme for his holiday. He was not going fishing or hunting this time—no, he had thought out a better plan. Out of his $40 a month he had saved enough for his purpose, in an economical way, and he was going to have a look at New York.

It was a great and surprising idea. It meant travel—immense travel—in those days it meant seeing the world; it was the equivalent of a voyage around it in ours. At first the other youths thought his mind was affected, but when they found that he was in earnest, the next thing to be thought of was, what sort of opportunity this venture might afford for a practical joke.

The young men studied over the matter, then held a secret consultation and made a plan. The idea was, that one of the conspirators should offer Ed a letter of introduction to Commodore Vanderbilt, and trick him into delivering it. It would be easy to do this. But what would Ed do when he got back to Memphis? That was a serious matter. He was good-hearted, and had always taken the jokes patiently; but they had been jokes which did not humiliate him, did not bring him to shame; whereas, this would be a cruel one in that way, and to play it was to meddle with fire; for with all his good nature, Ed was a Southerner—and the English of that was, that when he came back he would kill as many of the conspirators as he could before falling himself. However, the chances must be taken—it wouldn't do to waste such a joke as that.

So the letter was prepared with great care and elaboration. It was signed Alfred Fairchild, and was written in an easy and friendly spirit. It stated that the bearer was the bosom friend of the writer's son, and was of good parts and sterling character, and it begged the Commodore to be kind to the young stranger for the writer's sake. It went on to say, 'You may have forgotten me, in this long stretch of time, but you will easily call me back out of your boyhood memories when I remind you of how we robbed old Stevenson's orchard that night; and how, while he was chasing down the road after us, we cut across the field and doubled back and sold his own apples to his own cook for a hatfull of doughnuts; and the time that we—' and so forth and so on, bringing in names of imaginary comrades, and detailing all sorts of wild and absurd and, of course, wholly imaginary schoolboy pranks and adventures, but putting them into lively and telling shape.

With all gravity Ed was asked if he would like to have a letter to Commodore Vanderbilt, the great millionaire. It was expected that the question would astonish Ed, and it did.

> 'What? Do *you* know that extraordinary man?'
> 'No; but my father does. They were schoolboys together. And if you like, I'll write and ask father. I know he'll be glad to give it to you for my sake.'

Ed could not find words capable of expressing his gratitude and delight. The three days passed, and the letter was put into his hands. He started on his trip, still pouring out his thanks while he shook good-bye all around. And when he was out of sight his comrades let fly their laughter in a storm of happy satisfaction— and then quieted down, and were less happy, less satisfied. For the old doubts as to the wisdom of this deception began to intrude again.

Arrived in New York, Ed found his way to Commodore Vanderbilt's business quarters, and was ushered into a large anteroom, where a score of people were patiently awaiting their turn for a two-minute interview with the millionaire in his private office. A servant asked for Ed's card, and got the letter instead. Ed was sent for a moment later, and found Mr. Vanderbilt alone, with the letter—open—in his hand.

'Pray sit down, Mr.—er—'
'Jackson.'
'Ah—sit down, Mr. Jackson. By the opening sentences it seems to be a letter from an old friend. Allow me—I will run my eye through it. He says—he says—why, who is it?'

He turned the sheet and found the signature.

'Alfred Fairchild—hm—Fairchild—I don't recall the name. But that is nothing—a thousand names have gone from me. He says—he says—hm—hm—oh, dear, but it's good! Oh, it's rare! I don't quite remember it, but I seem to—it'll all come back to me presently. He says—he says—hm—hm—oh, but that was a game! Oh, splendid! How it carries me back! It's all dim, of course—it's a long time ago—and the names—some of the names are wavery and indistinct—but sho', I know it happened—I can feel it! And lord, how it warms my heart, and brings back my lost youth! Well, well, well, I've got to come back into this work-a-day world now—business presses and people are waiting—I'll keep the rest for bed to-night, and live my youth over again. And you'll thank Fairchild for me when you see him—I used to call him Alf, I think—and you'll give him my gratitude for what this letter has done for the tired spirit of a hard-worked man; and tell him there isn't anything that I can do for him or any friend of his that I won't do. And as for you, my lad, you are my guest; you can't stop at any hotel in New York. Sit where you are a little while, till I get through with these people, then we'll go home. I'll take care of you, my boy—make yourself easy as to that.'

Ed stayed a week, and had an immense time—and never suspected that the Commodore's shrewd eye was on him, and that he was daily being weighed and measured and analyzed and tried and tested.

Yes, he had an immense time; and never wrote home, but saved it all up to tell when he should get back. Twice, with proper modesty and decency, he proposed to end his visit, but the Commodore said, 'No—wait; leave it to me; I'll tell you when to go.'

In those days the Commodore was making some of those vast combinations of his—consolidations of warring odds and ends of railroads into harmonious systems, and concentrations of floating and rudderless commerce in effective centers—and among other things his far-seeing eye had detected the convergence of that huge tobacco-commerce, already spoken of, toward Memphis, and he had resolved to set his grasp upon it and make it his own.

The week came to an end. Then the Commodore said:

> 'Now you can start home. But first we will have some more talk about that tobacco matter. I know you now. I know your abilities as well as you know them yourself—perhaps better. You understand that tobacco matter; you understand that I am

going to take possession of it, and you also understand the plans which I have matured for doing it. What I want is a man who knows my mind, and is qualified to represent me in Memphis, and be in supreme command of that important business—and I appoint you.'

'Me!'

'Yes. Your salary will be high—of course—for you are representing me. Later you will earn increases of it, and will get them. You will need a small army of assistants; choose them yourself—and carefully. Take no man for friendship's sake; but, all things being equal, take the man you know, take your friend, in preference to the stranger.'

After some further talk under this head, the Commodore said:

> 'Good-bye, my boy, and thank Alf for me, for sending you to me.'

When Ed reached Memphis he rushed down to the wharf in a fever to tell his great news and thank the boys over and over again for thinking to give him the letter to Mr. Vanderbilt. It happened to be one of those idle times. Blazing hot noonday, and no sign of life on the wharf. But as Ed threaded his way among the freight piles, he saw a white linen figure stretched in slumber upon a pile of grain-sacks under an awning, and said to himself, 'That's one of them,' and hastened his step; next, he said, 'It's Charley—it's Fairchild—good'; and the next moment laid an affectionate hand on the sleeper's shoulder. The eyes opened lazily, took one glance, the face blanched, the form whirled itself from the sack-pile, and in an instant Ed was alone and Fairchild was flying for the wharfboat like the wind!

Ed was dazed, stupefied. Was Fairchild crazy? What could be the meaning of this? He started slow and dreamily down toward the wharfboat; turned the corner of a freight-pile and came suddenly upon two of the boys. They were lightly laughing over some pleasant matter; they heard his step, and glanced up just as he discovered them; the laugh died abruptly; and before Ed could speak they were off, and sailing over barrels and bales like hunted deer. Again Ed was paralyzed. Had the boys all gone mad? What *could* be the explanation of this extraordinary conduct? And so, dreaming along, he reached the wharfboat, and stepped aboard—nothing but silence there, and vacancy. He crossed the deck, turned the corner to go down the outer guard, heard a fervent 'O lord!' and saw a white linen form plunge overboard. The youth came up coughing and strangling, and cried out—

> 'Go 'way from here! You let me alone. I didn't do it, I swear I didn't!'
>
> 'Didn't do *what?*'
>
> 'Give you the—'
>
> 'Never mind what you didn't do—come out of that! What makes you all act so? What have I done?'
>
> 'You? Why *you* haven't done anything. But—'
>
> 'Well, then, what have you got against me? What do you all treat me so for?'

'I—er—but haven't you got anything against *us*?'

'Of course not. What put such a thing into your head?'

'Honor bright—you haven't?'

'Honor bright.'

'Swear it!'

'I don't know what in the *world* you mean, but I swear it, anyway.'

'And you'll shake hands with me?'

'Goodness knows I'll be *glad* to! Why, I'm just starving to shake hands with *somebody*!'

The swimmer muttered—

'Hang him, he smelt a rat and never delivered the letter!—but it's all right, I'm not going to fetch up the subject.'

And he crawled out and came dripping and draining to shake hands. First one and then another of the conspirators showed up cautiously—armed to the teeth—took in the amicable situation, then ventured warily forward and joined the love-feast.

And to Ed's eager inquiry as to what made them act as they had been acting, they answered evasively, and pretended that they had put it up as a joke, to see what he would do. It was the best explanation they could invent at such short notice. And each said to himself,

'He never delivered that letter, and the joke is on *us*, if he only knew it or we were dull enough to come out and tell.'

Then, of course, they wanted to know all about the trip; and he said—

'Come right up on the boiler deck and order the drinks—it's my treat. I'm going to tell you all about it. And to-night it's my treat again—and we'll have oysters and a time!'

When the drinks were brought and cigars lighted, Ed said:

'Well, when, I delivered the letter to Mr. Vanderbilt—'

'Great Scott!'

'Gracious, how you scared me. What's the matter?'

'Oh—er—nothing. Nothing—it was a tack in the chair-seat,' said one.

'But you *all* said it. However, no matter. When I delivered the letter—'

'*Did* you deliver it?'

And they looked at each other as people might who thought that maybe they were dreaming.

Then they settled to listening; and as the story deepened and its marvels grew, the amazement of it made them dumb, and the interest of it took their breath. They hardly uttered a whisper during two hours, but sat like petrifactions and drank in the immortal romance. At last the tale was ended, and Ed said—

'And it's all owing to *you*, boys, and you'll never find *me* ungrateful—bless your hearts, the best friends a fellow ever had! You'll all have places; I want every one of you. I *know* you—I know you "by the *back*", as the gamblers say. You're jokers, and all that, but you're *sterling*, with the hallmark *on*. And Charley Fairchild, you shall be my first assistant and right hand, because of your first-class ability, and because you got me the letter, and for your father's sake who wrote it for me, and to please Mr. Vanderbilt, who *said* it would! And here's to that great man—drink hearty!'

Yes, when the Moment comes, the Man appears—even if he is a thousand miles away, and has to be discovered by a practical joke.

20

A Parrot with an Acquired Taste

> When people do not respect us
> we are sharply offended; yet deep down
> in his private heart no man much
> respects himself.
>
> —*Pudd'nhead Wilson's New Calendar*

Necessarily, the human interest is the first interest in the log-book of any country. The annals of Tasmania whose shadow we were sailing, are lurid with that feature. Tasmania was a convict-dump, in old times; this has been indicated in the account of the Conciliator, where reference is made to vain attempts of desperate convicts to win permanent freedom, after escaping from Macquarrie Harbor and the 'Gates of Hell.' In the early days Tasmania had a great population of convicts, of both sexes and all ages, and a bitter hard life they had. In one spot there was a settlement of juvenile convicts—children—who had been sent thither from their home and their friends on the other side of the globe to expiate their 'crimes.'

In due course our ship entered the estuary called the Derwent, at whose head stands Hobart, the capital of Tasmania. The Derwent's shores furnish scenery of an interesting sort. The historian Laurie, whose book, *The Story of Australasia*, is just out, invoices its features with considerable truth and intemperance: 'The marvelous picturesqueness of every point of view, combined with the clear balmy atmosphere and the transparency of the ocean depths, must have delighted and deeply impressed' the early explorers.

> If the rockbound coasts, sullen, defiant, and lowering, seemed uninviting, these were occasionally broken into charmingly alluring coves floored with golden sand, clad with evergreen shrubbery, and adorned with every variety of indigenous wattle, she-oak, wild flower, and fern, from the delicately graceful 'maiden-hair' to the palm-like 'old man'; while the majestic gum tree, clean and smooth as the mast of 'some tall ammiral,' pierces the clear air to the height of two hundred and thirty feet or more.

It looks so to me.

Coasting along Tasman's Peninsula, what a shock of pleasant wonder must have struck the early mariner on suddenly sighting Cape Pillar, with its cluster of black-ribbed basaltic columns rising to a height of nine hundred feet, the hydra heads wreathed in a turban of fleecy cloud, the base lashed by jealous waves spouting angry fountains of foam.

That is well enough, but I did not suppose those snags were nine hundred feet high. Still they were a very fine show. They stood boldly out by themselves, and made a fascinatingly odd spectacle. But there was nothing about their appearance to suggest the heads of a hydra. They looked like a row of lofty slabs with their upper ends tapered to the shape of a carving-knife point; in fact, the early voyager, ignorant of their great height, might have mistaken them for a rusty old rank of piles that had sagged this way and that out of the perpendicular.

The Peninsula is lofty, rocky, and densely clothed with scrub, or brush, or both. It is joined to the main by a low neck. At this junction was formerly a convict station called Port Arthur—a place hard to escape from. Behind it was the wilderness of scrub, in which a fugitive would soon starve; in front was the narrow neck, with a cordon of chained dogs across it, and a line of lanterns, and a fence of living guards, armed. We saw the place as we swept by—that is, we had a glimpse of what we were told was the entrance to Port Arthur. The glimpse was worth something, as a remembrancer, but that was all.

> The voyage thence up the Derwent Frith displays a grand succession of fairy visions, in its entire length elsewhere unequaled. In gliding over the deep blue sea studded with lovely islets luxuriant to the water's edge, one is at a loss which scene to choose

for contemplation and to admire most. When the Huon and Bruni have been passed, there seems no possible chance of a rival; but suddenly Mount Wellington, massive and noble like his brother Etna, literally heaves in sight, sternly guarded on either hand by Mounts Nelson and Rumney; presently we arrive at Sullivan's Cove—Hobart!

It is an attractive town. It sits on low hills that slope to the harbor—a harbor that looks like a river, and is as smooth as one. Its still surface is pictured with dainty reflections of boats and grassy banks and luxuriant foliage. Back of the town rise highlands that are clothed in woodland loveliness, and over the way is that noble mountain, Wellington, a stately bulk, a most majestic pile. How beautiful is the whole region, for form, and grouping, and opulence, and freshness of foliage, and variety of color, and grace and shapeliness of the hills, the capes, the promontories; and then, the splendor of the sunlight, the dim rich distances, the charm of the water-glimpses! And it was in this paradise that the yellow-liveried convicts were landed, and the Corps-bandits quartered, and the wanton slaughter of the kangaroo-chasing black innocents consummated on that autumn day in May, in the brutish old time. It was all out of keeping with the place, a sort of bringing of heaven and hell together.

The remembrance of this paradise reminds me that it was at Hobart that we struck the head of the procession of Junior Englands. We were to encounter other sections of it in New Zealand, presently, and others later in Natal. Wherever the exiled Englishman can find in his new home resemblances to his old one, he is touched to the marrow of his being; the love that is in his heart inspires his imagination, and these allied forces transfigure those resemblances into authentic duplicates of the revered originals. It is beautiful, the feeling which works this enchantment, and it compels one's homage; compels it, and also compels one's assent—compels it always—even when, as happens sometimes, one does not see the resemblances as clearly as does the exile who is pointing them out.

The resemblances do exist, it is quite true; and often they cunningly approximate the originals—but after all, in the matter of certain physical patent rights there is only one England. Now that I have sampled the globe, I am not in doubt. There is a beauty of Switzerland, and it is repeated in the glaciers and snowy ranges of many parts of the earth; there is a beauty of the fiord, and it is repeated in New Zealand and Alaska; there is a beauty of Hawaii, and it is repeated in ten thousand islands of the Southern seas; there is a beauty of the prairie and the plain, and it is repeated here and there in the earth; each of these is worshipful, each is perfect in its way, yet holds no monopoly of its beauty; but that beauty which is England is alone—it has no duplicate. It is made up of very simple details —just grass, and trees, and shrubs, and roads, and hedges, and gardens, and houses, and vines, and churches, and castles, and here and there a ruin—and over it all a mellow dream-haze of history. But its beauty is incomparable, and all its own.

Hobart has a peculiarity—it is the neatest town that the sun shines on; and I incline to believe that it is also the cleanest. However that may be, its supremacy in neatness is not to be questioned. There cannot be another town in the world that has no shabby exteriors; no rickety gates and fences, no neglected houses crumbling to ruin, no crazy and unsightly sheds, no weed-grown front yards of the poor, no back yards littered with tin cans and old boots and empty bottles, no rubbish in the gutters, no clutter on the sidewalks, no outer borders fraying out into dirty lanes and tin-patched huts. No, in Hobart all the aspects are tidy, and all a comfort to the eye; the modestest cottage looks combed and brushed, and has its vines, its flowers, its neat fence, its neat gate, its comely cat asleep on the window ledge.

We had a glimpse of the museum, by courtesy of the American gentleman who is curator of it. It has samples of half a dozen different kinds of marsupials—one, the 'Tasmanian devil'; that is, I *think* he was one of them.[1] And there was a fish with lungs. When the water dries up it can live in the mud. Most curious of all was a parrot that kills sheep. On one great sheep-run this bird killed a thousand sheep in a whole year. He doesn't want the whole sheep, but only the kidney-fat. This restricted taste makes him an expensive bird to support. To get the fat he drives his beak in and rips it out; the wound is mortal. This parrot furnishes a notable example of evolution brought about by changed conditions. When the sheep culture was introduced, it presently brought famine to the parrot by exterminating a kind of grub which had always hitherto been the parrot's diet. The miseries of hunger made the bird willing to eat raw flesh, since it could get no other food, and it began to pick remnants of meat from sheep-skins hung out on the fences to dry. It soon came to prefer sheep meat to any other food, and by and by it came to prefer the kidney-fat to any other detail of the sheep. The parrot's bill was not well shaped for digging out the fat, but Nature fixed that matter; she altered the bill's shape, and now the parrot can dig out kidney-fat better than the Chief Justice of the Supreme Court, or anybody else, for that matter—even an Admiral.

And there was another curiosity—quite a stunning one, I thought: Arrow-heads and knives just like those which Primeval Man made out of flint, and thought he had done such a wonderful thing—yes, and has been humored and coddled in that superstition by this age of admiring scientists until there is probably no living with him in the other world by now. Yet here is his finest and nicest work exactly duplicated in our day; and by people who have never heard of him or his works: by aborigines who lived in the islands of these seas, within our time. And they not only duplicated those works of art but did it in the brittlest and most treacherous of substances—*glass*: made them out of old brandy bottles flung out of the British camps; millions of tons of them. It is time for Primeval Man to make a little less noise, now. He has had his day. He is not what he used to be.

We had a drive through a bloomy and odorous fairyland, to the Refuge for the Indigent—a spacious and comfortable home, with hospitals, etc., for both sexes. There was a crowd there, of the oldest people I have ever seen. It was like being suddenly set down in a new world—a weird world where Youth has never been, a world sacred to Age, and bowed forms, and wrinkles. Out of the 359 persons present, 223 were ex-convicts, and could have told stirring tales, no doubt, if they had been minded to talk; 42 of the 359 were past 80, and several were close upon 90; the average age at death there is 76 years. As for me, I have no use for that place; it is too healthy. Seventy is old enough—after that, there is too much risk. Youth and gaiety might vanish, any day—and then, what is left? Death in life; death without its privileges, death without its benefits. There were 185 women in that Refuge, and 81 of them were ex-convicts.

The steamer disappointed us. Instead of making a long visit at Hobart, as usual, she made a short one. So we got but a glimpse of Tasmania, and then moved on.

AFTERWORD

Mark Twain on the Platform
From: The Sketch, *27 November, 1895*

Unfortunately, perhaps, for himself, but decidedly fortunately for the people who have the pleasure of listening to him, Mark Twain has been dragged out of his American study by pecuniary losses to the footlights of the lecture-platform and the admiring gaze of his multitudinous readers. It is quite twenty years since the author of *Huck Finn* spoke across the footlights, and even at that distant date his lectures were very few in number, so that the people who have seen or heard the humorist in public prior to his present lecturing tour must be very limited indeed. Perhaps it is a good thing that Mark has been compelled to take to lecturing for a time, as it will enable him to visit countries previously unknown to him, and, as he has already promised, result in *Tramp Abroad*, Vol. II., being published. In fact, Mark Twain has so arranged his tour that he will not revisit any of the countries which formed such excellent scope for witty observation in his well-known book. Mark Twain placed himself unreservedly under the care of that well-known Colonial lecture-agent, Mr. R. S. Smythe, who has negotiated so many big 'stars' through the Colonies. Crossing from San Francisco, the humorist opened his tour in Sydney in the middle of September. His tour, which will last a year extends over all the Australian Colonies, New Zealand, Mauritius, Ceylon and South Africa. He had an offer of £2000 for ten lectures in London, but for the present had to refuse it. He will finish his Colonial tour, and get the resultant book off his hands before thinking of a trip to England.

As a lecturer—or rather, storyteller, for the author objects to be called a lecturer—Mark Twain is, and has proved himself to be, in his opening Australian 'At Homes,' a decided success. Like Charles Dickens, he relies entirely on his old books for the pabulum of his discourses, but, unlike the author of *Pickwick*, he does not read long extracts from these books. He takes some of his best stories—*The Jumping Frog, Huck Finn*, the difficulties of the German language, par exemple—and retells them, with many subtle additions of humour and some fresh observations, in the most irresistibly amusing manner. He is in no sense a disappointment as a humorist. He starts his audience laughing in the very first sentence he utters, and for two hours keeps them in a continual roar. The only serious moments occur when, with the unutterable pathos of which the true humorist alone is capable, he interpolates a few pathetic touches which almost make the tears mingle with the smiles. Every story he tells serves the purpose of illustrating a moral, and, although, for the most part, he talks in low, slow, conversational tones, at times he rises to real bursts of eloquence—not the polished, grandiloquent eloquence of the average American speaker, but the eloquence conveyed in simple words and phrases, and prompted by some deep and sincerely felt sentiment. The author has the power of seeming to jest at his serious side, just as in his books; but there is no mistaking the seriousness with which, for example, he is moved by the remembrance of the iniquities perpetrated on liberty in the old slavery days amid which Huck Finn and Jim the slave lived. He makes the most unexpected anecdotes point the most unexpected morals, but it is the recital of the old, familiar stories without any moral attaching to them which pleases most, coming as they do warm from the brain of the man who invented them.

Mark Twain steals unobtrusively on to the platform, dressed in the regulation evening-clothes, with the trouser-pockets cut high up into which he occasionally dives both hands. He bows with quiet dignity to the roaring cheers which greet him at every 'At Home.' Then with natural, unaffected gesture, and with scarcely any prelude, he gets under weigh with his first story. He is a picturesque figure on the stage. His long, shaggy, white hair surmounts a face full of intellectual fire. The eyes, arched with bushy brows, and which seem to be closed most of the time while he is speaking, flash out now and then from their deep sockets with a genial, kindly, pathetic look, and the face is deeply drawn with the furrows accumulated during an existence of sixty years. He talks in short sentences, with a peculiar smack of the lips at the end of each. His language is just that of his books, full of the quaintest Americanism, showing an utter disregard for the polished diction of most lecturers. 'It was not' is always 'twarn't' with Mark Twain, and 'mighty fine' and 'my kingdom' and 'they done it' and 'catched,' and various other purely transatlantic words and phrases, crop up profusely during his talk. He speaks slowly, lazily, and wearily, as of a man dropping off to sleep, rarely raising his voice above a conversational tone; but it has that characteristic nasal sound which penetrates to the back of the largest building. His figure is rather slight, not above middle height, and the whole man suggests an utter lack of physical energy. As a matter of fact, Mark Twain detests exercise, and the attraction must be very strong to induce him to go very far out of doors. Rolf Boldrewood called on him in Melbourne, and had the greatest difficulty in the world to persuade him to take a drive. With the exception of an occasional curious trot, as when recounting his buck-jumping experiences, Mark Twain stands perfectly still in one place during the whole of the time he is talking to the audience. He rarely moves his arms, unless it is with the right arm across the abdomen and the left resting on it and supporting his chin. In this way he talks on for nearly two hours; and while the audience is laughing uproariously, he never by any chance relapses into a smile. To have read Mark Twain is a delight, but to have seen and heard him is a joy not readily to be forgotten. The humorist is accompanied on his tour by his wife and charming second daughter.

—R. B. C

Notes

2. Intemperance Everywhere

1 J. S. Laurie, *The Story of Australasia: Its discovery, colonisation and development*, McIlvaine & Co., London, 1896.

3. Sydney—English City with American Trimmings

1 Douglas M. Gane, *New South Wales and Victoria in 1885*, Sampson Low, Marston, Searle & Rivington, London 1886.

9. To Adelaide

1 'The value of England's annual exports and imports is stated at three billions of dollars' was originally cited as information from the *New South Wales Blue Book*, a yearly government periodical (year not given). The text, 'it is claimed that more than one-tenth of this great aggregate is represented by Australasia's exports to England and imports from England' was originally cited as information from D. M. Luckie. No other information was given in the original text.
2 D. M. Luckie was cited as the source of this text. No other information was given in the original text.

11. The Laughing Jackass

1 The greatest heat in Victoria, that there is an authoritative record of, was at Sandhurst, in January, 1862. The thermometer then registered 117 degrees in the shade. In January, 1880, the heat at Adelaide, South Australia, was 172 degrees in the sun.
2 All but the last two distances are taken from George R. Parkin's *From Round the Empire*, Cassell, New York, 1892.

20. A Parrot with an Acquired Taste

1 A marsupial is a plantigrade vertebrate whose specialty is its pocket. In some countries it is extinct, in the others it is rare. The first American marsupials were Stephen Girard, Mr. Astor, and the opossum; the principal marsupials of the Southern Hemisphere are Mr. Rhodes and the kangaroo. I, myself, am the latest marsupial. Also, I might boast that I have the largest pocket of them all. But there is nothing in that.